CARNAC

The Life-Bringer

The Story of a Dawn Man
Told by Himself

***

Interpreted by

OLIVER MARBLE GALE

With a Foreword by

DR. ALFRED V. KIDDER

Explorer in Colorado and New Mexico for the
Archæological Institute of America, and Conductor
of Excavations for the University of Utah, Har-
vard University and Phillips Academy, Andover.

Illustrations in Color by Armstrong Sperry

Pictolith Sketches by Olive Otis

***

1928

WM. H. WISE & CO.

NEW YORK

Printed in the United States of America by
J. J. LITTLE AND IVES COMPANY, NEW YORK

CARNACK LEAPS UPWARD TERRIFIED. LOOF BOUNDS TO HIS
FEET, STIFF AND BRISTLING, FANGS SHOWING.

DEDICATED
TO
ALL THE CARNACKS
OF ALL TIME

CONTENTS

LIST OF ILLUSTRATIONS

7

CARNACK

FOREWORD

I READ the early chapters of *Carnack* with rising indignation. "When this pernicious book
gets published," thought I, "it is going to be taken
as gospel truth by nine-tenths of the people who
read it, and we shall have a worse myth than
Atlantis on our hands."

That was a first impression and, I believe, any
other archæologist would have reacted similarly—at
first. For archæologists have to be so constantly at
war with the public's fatal avidity for Lost Tribes
of Israel, for miraculous migrations of Egyptian
Sun-Priests, for fabled lands of gold and jewels,
that they develop a crabbed aversion to anything
not founded on the definite evidence of bones or
stones or potsherds.

But as a matter of fact there is all the difference
in the world between Carnack, the dawn man, and
Atlantis, the lost continent. Atlantis was not, nor
ever could have been, but Carnack did live and fight
and invent. You and I, who speak and write and
eat cooked food, prove his former existence by
everything we do, and in most of the things we
think. And that man, a weak and naked animal,
could have emerged triumphant from the million
hazards of the Pleistocene is surely far more wonderful than any single thing that he has since ac-

complished. Ancestral man, however, is separated
from us by such vast stretches of time, and he left
behind him relics so scanty, that he is to us but a
shadowy creature; we take his achievements for
granted, and we fail to realize the miracle of his
steady progress through the ages. Our palæolithic
forebears were folk well worth knowing, and did
we know them better we should be less interested
in the false marvels of legendary civilizations.

Carnack will bring much closer acquaintance.
The story is fundamentally true, because every
main event recorded in it has actually happened at
some time or place during the long slow evolution
of humanity. I should have been better pleased
had the scene been laid in Southern Asia, or perhaps in Central Africa, because it is reasonably
certain that the first steps in human progress were
not taken in the New World. But the book will
give many people who, very wisely, eschew the scientific journals, a most vivid glimpse of the childhood of man. They will enjoy it, or I am greatly
mistaken; and it may even lead some of them to dip
into Henry Fairfield Osborn and George Grant
MacCurdy. And that would be good for them and
for archæology.

A. V. K<small>IDDER</small>.

Andover, Mass.

Chapter I

I Discover a Life-Bringer

TWO hundred thousand years ago, and for thousands upon thousands of years theretofore and thereafter, human beings like ourselves, erect, self-conscious, seeming to themselves as important as we seem to ourselves, desiring as much as we do to continue to live and no doubt as confident as we are of the way they were doing it, actually did reside in caves and caverns in the rocks. Popular flippancies to that effect have one foot on the facts. Their history is now too well authenticated to be disputed or denied. Modern scientists, with indefatigable patience and inexorable penetration, have puzzled out their record from signs they left behind them in flints they scratched and scraped and slew out a living with, in bones of animals they feasted on in cave and camp, in pictures sculptured and painted on the walls they lived within, in their own fossil bones

13

found here and there beneath the débris of countless centuries which men have now learned how to count.

Huddled through long bitter winters in the dark recesses of their caves, scantily wrapped in stiff, stinking skins, rigid with cold, dumb with hunger; sleeping on foul beds of boughs, dried grass or musty rushes; subsisting precariously on the raw flesh of what animals they could kill by hand with hand-made weapons and on what nuts and berries and nutritious roots they could find; beset on every side by terrifying mystery, and with the plains and forests where they had to hunt their food infested with ferocious beasts of prey that hunted them, life as they saw it was nothing but a struggle to exist. Alone in the dusk of dawning human consciousness, having no others they might turn to for information, comfort or support and no help at hand, as they supposed, beyond the sticks and stones about them, they groped on amongst their rocks through the dull centuries with no concept of existence beyond a blind instinct to cling to it, no hope in it but to live a little longer in the same old way.

Yet the very rocks that sheltered them, the rivers running at their feet, the woods they hunted in, the air they breathed, the sun they saw by, were potential every hour with every convenience, safety, comfort and abundance that we enjoy today. The houses that we live in and the pipes that keep them piping hot; the clean, neat clothes we buy in shops and wear; the smooth, soft beds we lie in; the running water and the daily bath; the chosen food upon our tables and the telephone that brings it there; the cars we ride in and the movies that they take us to; the plays we go to see and the radio with which we stay at home, are not more possible to us today than they were to them. Nothing has changed but the thought of man; nothing is new but the spirit we see in him.

Not long ago a student friend of mine had a theme to write on the proverb: "Where there's a will, there's a way." "A glimpse at the various inventions and wonderful discoveries of the last decade or so leads us to believe that the only thing necessary to do or to make anything is to decide that you want it to be done," he begins. "Feats which the most learned of yesterday declared absolutely impossible are being performed by the most ignorant of today, through the efforts of the will more than the minds of some of our great men, and things which we have no idea can happen, will be happening tomorrow," he goes on.

Then, a bit playfully, but with an intuitive insight

and vision which makes it clear that his "theme" is not merely one of those fortuitous inspirations of a soul beyond its depth, he discusses the development of human intercommunication from the time when, as he assumes, "the first men probably conveyed their messages a la axe, club or fist," through the phenomenon of the radio to the achievement, not yet fully demonstrated, of "detecting thought waves."

"Where will it all end?" he concludes. "It won't end. For where there is a will there will always be a way. And there will always be the will—the will of God."

Here this young man, it seems to me, puts his thematic finger on the origin of all human progress. The will of God worketh continually that His children should come forth from the dark, cold caves of ignorance and fear and lack into the light of His countenance and the joy and abundance of their true selfhood as His children from the beginning, whom He loves and will not suffer always to be less in their own consciousness than they are in His. Human advance is the fruit of this divine urge overmastering the destiny of some man or woman and compelling him, or her, whether or no, to think new thoughts, do new deeds, speak new tongues. As

Paul puts it: "For it is God that worketh in us both to will and to do of His good pleasure."

These are the life-bringers.

Life-bringers are, as a rule, looked upon as nuisances. We want to be permitted to cling in peace to our old familiar caves of theology, politics, economics and the social order without being disturbed by the precedent or preaching of anyone who has found some new ones. We feel safe in them. We know our way about in them. We can be reasonably sure of what is going to happen in them, and what is not. We know where the bottomless pits are, and where we are likely to knock our heads against overhanging roofs or hit our knees on rough projections. We have acquainted ourselves with the habits and habitats of all the evil spirits that infest them, and can keep pretty much out of their way. We would be perfectly willing, of course, to have a cave without bottomless pits in it to tumble into and low rocks to knock our heads against and rough projections to stumble over in dark corners and evil spirits to frighten ourselves with; but how can we be confident that another cave would be better than this one?

We cannot; so we stick to the one we know about. We would rather be sure about an ascertained worst than be in suspense about a problematical best. We are afraid of what we cannot predetermine from past experiences that we have more or less survived. We want tomorrow to be as nearly as possible like today and yesterday, which we know we have come through alive. We try to wrap the future up in neat, familiar packages which we can put away on a shelf, catalogued and labeled, with a card index to them in the vault. Our idea of Heaven itself is a glorious and musical sort of a place where everything is over and nothing more can happen to us.

Whereas life is in fact a state of flux in which nothing is ever crystalized or finished; a ceaseless discard, renewal and refreshment; a forward march into unfoldment; a vast experiment with good; an endless experience with God Himself, Who is Life and Who gives it endlessly. To be on guard against a changing life is to ward off life itself; to miss the very point and purpose of existence.

It was this instinct of false self-preservation which, nineteen hundred years ago, sought to kill Christ Jesus, and thought that it had done so; and still tries daily to destroy him, without the slightest idea of what it is about. This most notable example in all history of one taking up the offensive against so-called life and aligning himself with the power behind all progress, individual and collective, expressing in its fulness both by demonstration and instruction the particular perfection and universal perfectibility which is the promise to those who fulfil all righteousness, frightened the defensive life so completely out of its senses that it wiped him out in a most effective way, as it supposed, by nailing him in person to a cross and afterwards distorting his doctrines into pleasant Sunday platitudes and a safety device for a future world. We see this false instinct lifting its terrified head throughout all ages in an attempt to save its own false sense of life. Adam and Eve were its first recorded victims. Abel succumbed to it in Cain. It threw Joseph into pit and prison. Christ Jesus himself called attention to what it inflicted on the prophets. And consider Saul of Tarsus, breathing out threatenings and slaughter, before his conversion made him Paul the Apostle.

Nor is the stake set up for the martyr in the field of religion alone. Hatred of the advancing idea has left the mark of the beast beside the road of all human progress, mental, moral, mechanical, scientific, social. Who dares yet point out whom it may have slain in our own day?

In peering down the dusky corridors of time we

observe it to be easier, on the whole, to entertain intelligent amazement at this resistance to life-bringers in proportion to the remoteness of each instance from our own time-point. We know perfectly well, for example, each of us, what would have been our personal attitude towards that obscure Jewish carpenter walking up and down the countryside addressing curious multitudes from fishing boats, daisy patches, street corners, and the houses of publicans and sinners. We know how we would have regarded the healing of all their diseases, the casting out of their deaf and dumb devils, and the raising of their dead. But when it comes to attempting to single out those of our contemporaries whom time will prove to have been true life-bringers from those restless and rebellious spirits on the one hand who would sweep everything into the dust-bin, the good with the bad, and the tinkering, platitudinous reformers on the other who run up and down nervously trying to fit all backs to their own hair shirts, we find it a different matter.

We know that those who whiffer and chaffer for a daily yeast are the whey and froth, the tumbling foam and hissing bubbles, atop the deep-bottomed billows of life that swing themselves ceaselessly against the self-crystalizing cliffs of human thought and habit. We know that the emotional intrusion of an egotistical morality and piousness by sentimental impertinents is a spurious substitute for the devoted introduction of a new idea which frees and regenerates. But we also know that we must be wary, for our own sakes, as well as theirs, to judge righteous judgment. For who is so wise as to discern the hand of God in the signs of the times?

Since our cave-dwelling predecessors were like ourselves in respect of being human, we can be very sure that one appeared amongst them now and then who was prompted by the divine urge we have been speaking of to enquire, for instance, whether there might not be some better form of shelter than a cold and smelly cave, or some better covering than the hard, hairy skins of animals. Or to introduce confusion and uncertainty by devising new flint instruments or new uses for old ones, which would have been perfectly acceptable if some one else, some one they all knew better, some older hunter, some chief man, had thought of them first; or by practicing some other method of discussion than club, tooth and claw.

We know that there must have been some such unsatisfied and enquiring spirits amongst them because the race no longer lives in that sort of cave.

So it should not seem so surprising that I ran across one out in Utah two or three summers ago.

I do not know how old, in terms of years, this sempiternal friend of mine should be said to be. Quite a dispute on that point, as well as on many others concerning him, has developed amongst archæologists, palentologists, geologists and the like. Some say he lived two hundred thousand years ago; some, fifty; others, twenty-five. A few hold him to have been even more recent, while some maintain he never existed at all.

Their arguments are technical and tedious, requiring special knowledge to be understood. Anyone caring to follow the discussion can find it in any good library amongst the transactions of learned societies, reports of museum expeditions, and in magazines devoted to prehistory. One man, I am told, has written a book on the subject.

I had not the slightest idea, when my hand rested on the piece of rock where his had left its trace, that I was in the very act of discovering prehistoric troglodytes in America, or the least suspicion of what a stir such a discovery would cause in scientific circles. Neither did I realize at the time that I had found a life-bringer. That dawned upon me later, as I came to know him better. I was, however, enormously stirred. I felt that something exciting had happened.

I encountered this ancient life-bringer on the face of a cliff in western Utah just before sunset one summer afternoon in 1924. We were motoring through, the boys and I, and while they made camp I had wandered off in search of some sequestered spot where I might permit myself to fancy that mine had been the first foot to press the rocks since their cooling, jellied masses had rumpled into form and firmness and that, throughout the succeeding solitary centuries, no other eye than mine had swept the scene.

This desire to be alone in the open solitudes of time and space is, I take it, a form of religious instinct common to us all. We experience, I think, at such a time, when our backs are turned upon the little matters that concern Him not and no one else is near to startle the rapport, a tremulous, exquisite consciousness of the First Cause, Who seems to come striding down the corridors of time to smile and speak to us alone. We step, for a moment, within the portals of pure spirit, sensible of Creator and creation, intimately aware of our place and part in Him, and His in us.

This desire and its fulfilment I understand to be

the ocean's fascination and the desert's lure; the
benediction of the silent woods, the mountain's inspiration and the spell of the prairie's wide expanse;
the glory of the setting sun; the whispered mystery
of magic midnight, and the exaltation of the stars.

All day long we had been forging across the
immemorial emptiness and primordial silence of the
basin country of Nevada and Utah. For hour on
solitary hour the only sign of man beside our hum-
ming car had been the tiny thread of road weaving
up through rocky ridges out of one basin and down
again to string out in a long, dusty ribbon across
the next. For mile upon interminable mile there
had been no spring of water or tree of green or running brook or living thing, save only bush on bush,
bush on bush, all alike in size and shape and color,
in delirious monotony.

So the mood to be alone was strong upon me.

We had stopped for the night on the edge of a
gigantic basin that seemed, after a long day, too
vast and empty to be undertaken before morning.
The road ahead of us struck off across the plain in
a straight track that dwindled out of sight in sheer
distance, still unswerving, on the farther slope. Beyond, the other rim of the basin swam rose-tipped
above the rising shadows of descending night.

Not far from where we had camped a desolate cañon debouched into the basin. I strolled over and began to ascend it. The chasm wound into the hills, untouched, untamed, enchanting. The bed was rough and steep and broken. Presently I found myself clinging to its walls. The going grew more difficult, but each step led me to the next one.

I was clambering along a shelf that amounted to little more than a series of scattered niches, admonished at every step by increasing acclivity and diminishing foothold to go no farther, when a flake of the vertical wall to which I was holding fast came away in my fingers, nearly pitching me into the cañon.

That, of course, settled it. . . .

But beyond the next point of rock, scarcely a dozen feet ahead of me, the country promised to open out into just such a spot as I was looking for.

I stopped to study a way across the intervening cliff. The flat flake of wall that had come away was still in my hand, as big as my palm, half an inch thick, or less.

I had picked out my route, step by step, and was about to toss the flat piece over the brink to watch it twist and flutter out of sight before I started

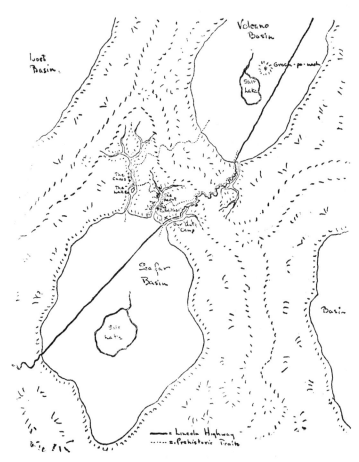

MAP OF SEAFAR AND VOLCANO BASINS. BETWEEN THEM IS
THE VALLEY OF THE CAVES TRAVERSED BY THE LINCOLN
HIGHWAY AND PREHISTORIC TRAILS, AS INDICATED.

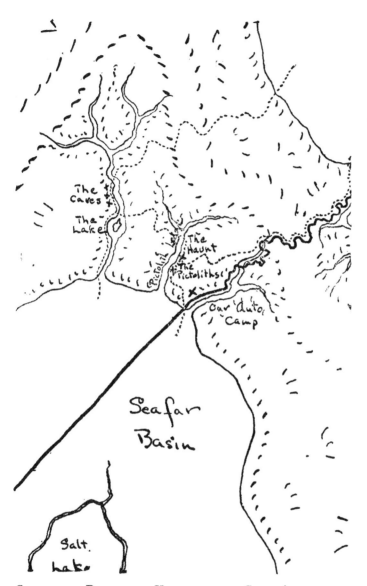

SHOWING IN DETAIL THE VALLEY OF THE CAVES ABUTTING ON
SEAFAR BASIN, THE LOCATION OF THE CAVES THEMSELVES
AND OTHER PREHISTORIC SITES.

across, when something on its surface caught my attention.

At first I took it to be a curious conformation of the rock's thin laminations, due to tricks of erosion.

But I soon saw that I was wrong. Amazingly wrong.

What I saw upon the rock was a drawing.

The unmistakable figure of a dog, half carved, half scratched, in the smooth surface, with the legs of a man sketched in behind.

Some one had been there before me.

I felt creepy.

I looked around.

Chapter II

He Creates a Disturbance

THUS came about a discovery of prehistoric man in western America which set by the ears the world of archæologists, palæontologists, anthropologists, ethnologists, geologists and what not. Discussion ran through field after field of scientific stubble with a mighty crackle and smoke, kindling one group after another into hot debate. Newspapers made a day's sensation of the lonely carver of the desert hills; sermons were preached on him, articles written. Fundamentalists condemned the man and those who had found him; evolutionists pointed to him with a new finality. When popular curiosity was at its height a new wonder appeared in the sky and scientific circles, badly pulled awry the while, were allowed to return to their proper centers and circumferences. There the discussion still continues; or did, when last I heard of it.

Learned men produced from caves in France and Spain chipped flints and carved reindeer horns and parietal paintings and I know not what talk about

Cro-Magnon and Aurignacian and Solutrian to
show that no people could have arrived at the stage
of culture necessary to the production of even the
most primitive art at the place in question within
the time limits rigidly laid down by the geologists.
Three hundred and forty-two stone pictures like
the first which I laid before them with the naïve enthusiasm of a child they swept aside as fortuitous or
forged, without bothering to explain by what acci-
dents of nature so many intelligible graphic repre-
sentations could have been brought about in any
case, to say nothing of their being related to one
another, as they obviously were; or why any casual
itinerant hoaxer would have set his jocular trap in
so obscure and unlikely a place, where the chances
were all against its ever being sprung; or why, if
I myself had gone to the trouble of preparing them
as advance publicity for a book I intended to write,
I would have made the drawings so difficult to inter-
pret, as they will be seen to be.

Others, accepting the find at face value or pursuing investigations of their own, joined the skeptics
in vigorous issue, laboriously proving, point by
point, that the man they challenged could have existed, that he could have lived at the place in question within the geologists' time limits, and that he

might have had the intelligence and skill to make pictures in stone. While a few, maintaining what is known as the scientific attitude of mind, preferred to withold their opinions until further evidence on the pictoliths, as they were called, should be produced.

For my part, I kept aloof from the controversy after the first few exchanges had provoked me to take a hand in it. Rattling the bones and raising the dust of two hundred thousand years on two continents to determine the ethnological and cultural possibilities of the "reputed find" struck me as being a bit idle and beside the point, with the very life and soul of the man himself unfolding to me day by day out of the pictured rocks I held within my hand.

The attitude of the reluctant scientists is easily understood. My discovery was unheard of. No pictoliths like these had ever been found anywhere. No traces of the earliest cave life had ever before been encountered in America, to say nothing of western America or Utah. Neither ethnology, archæology, geology or any other ology furnished grounds for expecting that they would be; but on the contrary offered strong reasons for expecting that they would not. Furthermore, and the argument is valid, who was I?

I had not, as I have said, any intimation of all this while I stood there perched on the eyebrow of the precipice staring at the little flat piece of scratched rock in my hand. I did, however, feel the presence of a great antiquity. Hundreds of years, I thought, thousands, perhaps, had passed since the man who had been there before me stood upon that spot. The ecstatic loneliness for which I had been seeking came welling over me out of the deep pools of the past, floating me off on a pulseless sea without a shore. Slowly across the great gulf fixed between us we two saluted each other. The vanished centuries were bridged by a tiny flake of stone with lines upon it. He had made them; I had seen them. We stood on its dizzy span, two flecks, two atoms, measuring immeasurability. Yet my wildest guess was twelve score centuries too short!

Walter came upon me there with this man's handiwork within my hand gazing out across the empty reaches that the other's eye had once beheld. He had followed me, leaving Oliver to finish getting supper.

Half a dozen strides brought him to my elbow. I showed him the stone picture. He was not impressed at first. Then it dawned on him, and he gave me a look.

"Where did you find it?" he wanted to know.

I told him.

The boy, of course, turned to have a look at the place whence the picture had been plucked. "Oh, for heaven's sake!" he cried. "Look here!"

A great vertical slab of the wall, all that remained of it, was filled with similar drawings.

In our first excitement we were too hurried to make much of the pictures. They appeared to be random sketches, crude and meaningless. Then we began to perceive that some of them seemed to belong together. Here and there we traced out a more or less orderly arrangement. A few we were sure were in series. Before long we were identifying individuals who appeared in different pictures. One we knew by his size; another by his bent, squat legs—an exaggerated crook of the knees amounting almost to caricature—and heavy torso; a third, a young woman, by her features, drawn remarkably alike in every picture except for quaint, straight lines at various angles which we took to be intended to express human emotions—joy, fear, grief. A boy was obvious. Walter was certain that he traced another man through many pictures by an athletic development of the lower legs; the very legs we had found on the original fragment. It was not until later, when we had isolated several individuals, that I was able to determine beyond the shadow of a doubt that this was the artist himself.

There were many animals, and many kinds of animals; bison, elk, deer, bear, lions or some other large cat; horses, wolves, squirrels, hares, two or three species I did not recognize and which we later learned had become extinct; some birds I could not identify and some that I could. The dog of the first picture, distinguished by his size and strength, we found repeated frequently throughout more than half the rock. A single horse, separated from the herds, came into the picture towards the end.

Walter, scrabbling excitedly about in the detritus on the little shelves and ledges amongst which we clung, picked up more pictures on stone flakes like the one that had come off in my hand; some hopelessly fragmentary, some virtually intact. We were deeply stirred. We rattled on at a great rate with voices raised, shouting and laughing; but without the slightest understanding of what we really had found.

Never before had prehistoric drawings been discovered which represented action, depicted stories

or attempted portraiture—one of the reasons, by
the way, insisted on why those which we had come
upon could not be authentic. The nearest other
known approach to narrative or movement amongst
primeval pictures is an ivory engraving of a mam-
moth charging, found at La Madeleine, in France,
while the most pretentious dramatic scene previ-
ously revealed shows a small herd of reindeer crossing a stream with salmon swimming amongst their
legs. Another has a bit of unrelated landscape
sketched in—a tuft of reeds, apparently, at the
edge of water. Otherwise, even the most elaborate
and skillful of them are merely "still lifes" of single
animals without background or environment; while
facsimiles of humans are almost entirely wanting,
being confined to a few grotesques not unlike our
modern comic strips.

Whereas the pictoliths of Utah, as may be seen
from the reproductions of them in this book, are
story pictures of both animals and people, full of
action, drama, color, character—when you learn to
find these in them, as we did—and achieving even
landscape in repeated instances.

But what is more amazing than all this; what
leaves the scientists, trained to a limited expectancy
towards the disclosures of prehistory agog with

skeptical surprise and sends a tingle of romance
along the marrow of the layman's bones, is that,
as we peer steadily into these pictures we see a solitary, lonely man stir slowly into life far down the
crumbled galleries of time, emerge from their spec-
tral shadows and come marching forth upon us with
a gesture and a nod. For the Seafar Basin pictoliths are nothing more nor less than the autobiog-
raphy and memoirs of a man who lived and thought
and wrought twenty thousand years before the first
syllable of recorded time.

Oliver had to come and get us. He found us in
the growing dusk, after much halloing and wandering in wrong directions, buzzing up against the face
of the precipice like two great bumble bees.

Walter was all for coming back after supper with
the flashlight to finish up so that we would not be
delayed in the morning; whereupon I was obliged
to remind him, not for the first time, that motoring,
like life, consisted not alone in getting somewhere,
but in being where you were; and we all agreed that
we would spend the entire next day on the spot.

As a matter of fact, we remained there from that
night, which was Friday, until the following Tuesday noon on this, our first visit, and have returned
three times since. I have, at least; the boys were

unable to accompany me on the third expedition, made with Fischer, of the Hamburg Academy.

How to collect our pictures was the practical question that confronted us in the morning; for we had decided over night that we wanted to take them home with us. Walter thought that we could pry off a thin sheath of the wall bearing them and load it into the car, but we soon found that we could not split away the outer laminations without fracturing the pictures badly. Furthermore, it occurred to me that it might be best, in the interests of science, to leave them where they were until the experts might have had their fill of them.

Oliver solved the problem for us. He took sheets from my loose-leaf notebook, placed them against the smooth surface upon which the pictures were engraved, rubbed upon them with the leaden bullets of some revolver cartridges we had with us, as a small boy rubs with a pencil on a piece of paper laid over a coin, and brought off fairly good facsimiles. Being by nature a thoroughgoing, orderly and patient person, he eventually had, with our help, all the pictures on the wall copied, numbered and in order, with a diagram of the wall itself and the position on it of each picture in the group. This diagram proved to be invaluable in our studies;

without it the solution of the Seafar Basin pictoliths would scarcely have been possible.

This was a task. We had to rig him up against the face of the rock with the auto tow-line, to give him some freedom of movement for his arms, while he was doing it, and stand by for the most part to hand him his material and take care of the pictures as he brought them off. Now and then Walter took a turn at the work; but he put in his time with more enthusiasm and to better purpose, when he could be spared, ranging up and down the cliff beneath us, at the pleasurable risk of his neck, searching for spalled-off pieces of the pictured rock, of which we found enough, first and last, to make an appreciable load for the tonneau of the car.

It was on this first morning, while the boys were busy at their work, that I discovered The Haunt, as we came to call it. As soon as they were well started—Oliver rigged up in his rope, Walter standing by with paper, bullets and suggestions—I edged my way out towards the corner that I had been intent on negotiating the night before when the fragment broke off in my hand. Walter, catching sight of me flattened out against the precipice like a fly on a windy wall, scrambled over to help; but he was too late. Two quick, rather desperate

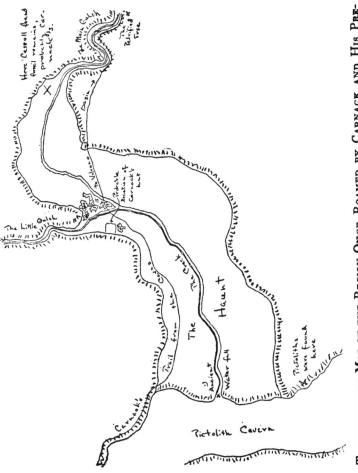

Here Carroll found
fossil remains,
probably Car-
nack's.

The Main Gulch

The Petrified River

Oasis

X

The Little Gulch

The Volcano

Probable
location of
Carnack's hut

Trail from the Cave

The Haunt

Carnack's

Trail from

Ancient
Water fall

Pictoliths
were found
here

Pictolith Cavern

TOPOGRAPHICAL MAP OF THE REGION ONCE ROAMED BY CARNACK AND HIS PRE-
HISTORIC TRIBEFOLK. SHOWING WHERE THE PICTOLITHS WERE DISCOVERED.

steps in mid-air and a hurried leap brought me safely over, and he went back to help his brother.

The country, as I had expected, opened up beyond this rocky shoulder; but I was not prepared for what unfolded to me. I was looking into a peaceful, almost verdant amphitheater a hundred yards or two in width, sloping gently from the abutting mountain walls to a little green thread that wound down through it, and reaching with slow, swinging double curves a mile or so into the hills, where it narrowed down into a gorge that climbed swiftly and soon twisted out of sight, affording, so we learned, an exit from the tiny mountain valley. Here and there were quiet nooks tucked in amongst the rocks. I observed a tree or two. There was a serenity about the place. It was absurd, of course, but a sense of that other consciousness had been so impressed upon me by the stone tablet just around the corner and the thought of him had wrought such a spell upon me that I more than half expected, as I stood looking up and down the valley and into every nook and corner of it, to see the man himself in skins and flints come striding towards me out of the centuries.

Half a day's inspection of the place revealed no trace to my unpracticed eye of human habitation,

present, past, or primitive; but it was in this very
valley, midway along its southern side, in a charming little spot where a tiny gulch still creeps down
out of the wall with a whispering spring between its
grassy lips, that Fischer, sent out by the Hamburg
Museum, found, lying beneath the casual debris of
twenty-five thousand mountain winters and desert
summers, fossil bones and flint arrow heads which
he maintains are traces of an ancient camp or resi-
dence. And it was at the head of this same cañon
that Cassell, of the Anthropological Institute, dis-
interred the fossilized remains of Carnack himself,
as I have called this life-bringer of two hundred
and fifty centuries ago. I, at least, have always
held them to be his, for reasons which seem to me to
be conclusive; but the identification is involved in
another technical controversy which has no place
here.

While we saw none of this, the boys and I, we did
identify this spot before we left on Tuesday noon
as a scene recurring in the pictoliths; a recognition
proved correct when both Fischer and Cassell
located, through the very drawings that we hit upon
as picturing the valley, the points within it where
their researches were rewarded by success.

It was not until the third expedition, made with

Fischer, the first scientist to respond to the opportunity which the announcement of the find had opened, after I had given much time to the study of the pictoliths, that the caves which appear in them so frequently were located. What remained of them, that is to say; which was no more than a geological trace hidden from the untrained observer but detected by M. Jules Perigord, a young French geologist, an amateur, who had accompanied Dr. Fischer at his own expense out of sheer enthusiasm over the possibilities promised by an unexploited discovery. For my part, I was long in seeing the signs in the hills themselves that caves had ever been there, having to take much on faith at first; although their presence at the precise site where Perigord placed them accorded to a line with the pictures, clearing up a question that had vexed me for months.

Before the expedition returned, however, it had uncovered evidence making it clear that the caves had been where Perigord from the first had placed them. At a low level in the talus about the foot of the cliff which he had designated as their site, fossil bones of certain extinct animals were found in such circumstances of juxtaposition with flint implements that we know the men that made the flints used the animals as food and were therefore contemporaneous with them. But these extinct animals Perigord showed to have existed within a period when, as he was also able to point out, men in that locality lived exclusively in caves. Wherefore the caves must have been at the point where the bones and flints were found together.

The observations and deductions by which Perigord arrived at his conclusions are so ingenious and engaging and afford such a pretty illustration of the manner in which these erudite gentlemen solve, from the slightest tangible grounds, the problems that confront them, that I have tried a dozen times at this point to go into them. But they are so intricate, so tenuous, and so highly technical at important steps in the argument, that I have been compelled to abandon the attempt. Each time I could scarcely make head or tail of what I had written, although I had had a fairly clear grasp of the subject myself when I began the exposition.

This same brilliant young Frenchman accounted for the smooth stone tablet on the cliff where the pictoliths were found. The rocky foliation was a thin verticle intrusion of fine-grained material pushed up through the softer rock about it. This harder foliation, outlasting its envelope, was left

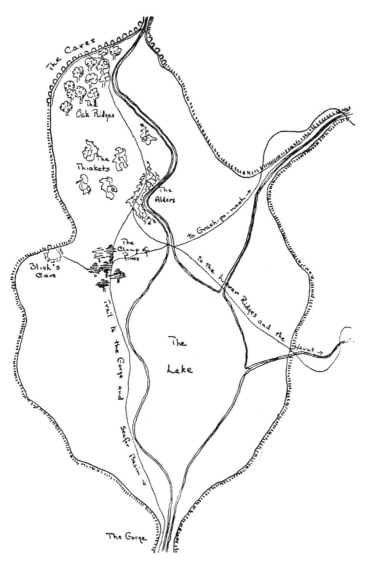

The Caves

The Oak Ridges

The Thickets

The Alders

to Grasshopper-nest

The Clump of Pines

Blish's Cave

To the Lower Ridges and the

Trail to the Gorge and Safe Basin

The Lake

Haunt

The Gorge

SHOWING THE LOCATION OF THE CAVES AND VARIOUS POINTS
OF INTEREST BETWEEN THEM AND THE GORGE.

standing as the softer formation eroded away. At the time of Carnack it formed a smooth, sheltered wall at the back of what was then a rather wide and gracious bench perched on the flank of the cañon; no doubt an altogether pleasant retreat, cool and airy and secluded, with a charming prospect.

Wind and water had gradually sliced this bench away from under foot as far back as the vertical stratification which at that prehistoric time was already exposed above the floor of the bench, a convenient canvas to the hand of the artist. Perigord pointed out to me the vast changes the region had undergone. Another hundred years, or a thousand, and this sheath of rock with its priceless record had gone the way of the rest, and the history of our life-bringer and his people had been lost forever.

Chapter III

He Becomes a Puzzle

THE reproductions in this book are chiefly from photographs of the pictoliths taken on our second expedition made later that same summer, while they were still in place. Others are copied direct from the fragments that we found lying about and took with us. Oliver's rub-offs, while serving for purposes of study until we got the better pictures, could not be used for reproduction. The outer lamination of the wall itself, bearing the pictoliths, has since been removed and carted off by the Cassell expedition, and is now undergoing intensive study at the Institute before being released for exhibition on the Institute's floors.

At first, naturally enough, I turned to the specialists for light on the pictures I had found and the man that made them. Those who regarded the entire business as a broad practical joke, perpetrated either by me or upon me, were obviously of little help. Nor were those who took the pictures seriously of much more assistance. Beyond placing the time somewhere between twenty thousand and two hundred thousand years ago, and determining from collateral evidence discovered later and repudiated by the conservatives that he probably understood the use of fire and the bow, and may have domesticated the dog—all of which the pictures themselves show—their speculations have been of little real value in the study of the man himself. What sort he was, how he lived, what he thought and felt, they told me were matters of pure conjecture and inference, my conjectures and inferences being as valid as theirs; a conclusion to which I had come independently of them long before.

The interpretation of the now famous Seafar Basin Pictoliths set forth in this volume was not the work of a day. Not only did the riddle of each individual picture have to be read, but it had to be read in conjunction with and relation to every other picture and the entire group. But the meaning and arrangement of the entire group depended upon the meaning and the position of each picture forming the group. To learn what each meant and where it belonged one must know what all meant and where they belonged; while to ascertain what all meant and determine their order one must penetrate to the meaning and fix the position of each one.

By what slow-footed spirals this recurrent cycle was straightened out and the riddle read at last; by what hard-won glimpses here into some obscurity of line or composition and what sudden flashes there revealing whole groups of pictures in one instant's vision; by what fantastic guesses subsequently seen to be correct and what logical deductions brought to naught; what ingenious theories applied and laid aside; what easygoing high roads followed to no thoroughfares, what devious, inconsequential lanes explored and discovered to be highways paved with information, I will not stop to tell. Fascinating as the work was in itself, with its mental challenge and tussle, its suspenses and surprises, its curiosity piqued and its expectations baffled, its secrets whispering and rustling just around each tantalizing corner, and above all its intensely human thrill in repeatedly coming face to face with living men and women twenty-five thousand years old, a detailed account of it would, I am sure, prove tedious here. Other interpretations of the pictoliths, of course, are possible, and no doubt will be forthcoming; but I am sure that this one is in

general a true and just account of the life of Carnack and his people.

The first picture found was one of the most difficult, perhaps, that we encountered. The dog was
distinct enough, and the man's legs were perfectly
plain; but why the picture, and why was it on the
upper edge of the tablet, whence my fingers had
inadvertently plucked it? From its location at that
point it should have celebrated some early episode
or circumstance in the artist's life. But the dog, or
wolf, depicted in it does not appear in other pictures
until the story is well under way.

Oliver hit upon the solution. He suggested that
the position of the dog at the head of the record was
a question of importance rather than of sequence.
Of importance, at least, in the eyes of Carnack. A
study of the pictures as a whole bears out this conclusion. Other events in the career of our life-
bringer may seem to us to be of greater moment to
himself and to his people than his domestication of
the wolf, but it is not difficult to see how the half-
wild companionship which he found and formed in
the lonely hills of Utah with a leader of the pack
at a time when his own fellows were already beginning to drive him out, loomed large to him.

The nature of the animal itself has been vigor-

ously disputed. Some assert it to be a wolf out
and out; others, a downright dog; while still others
maintain it to be a wolf in process of becoming a
dog. Despite the weight of scientific opinion which
today denies to the dog a lupine origin and refuses
the wolf canine posterity, this is my view, forced
upon me and sustained by the part the animal plays
in the life of Carnack and the part that Carnack
plays in his.

The caves where Carnack lived with his people
—we have no way, of course, of knowing his name;
Carnack and all the others are pure invention—
were located by Perigord, the young French geologist, at the base of a red sandstone cliff at the
upper end of a broad, level mountain valley about
five miles from The Haunt, where the close-press-
ing hills relaxed their grip on the stream wriggling
to escape between them and wheeled aside in wide,
parenthetical sweeps, converging again miles below in a formidable, rocky gorge.

Carnack's pictoliths, as well as geology, tell us
that these caves were not like those of France and
Spain, where so much prehistory has been traced,
which were formed by water melting out of glacial
ice on the plains behind the rivers and flowing down
through cracks in the limestone plateaus until long

labyrinthine caverns had been worn out, dark and fantastic, with openings in the palisades of the river banks. The caves of Utah were hollowed into the soft foot of the sandstone cliffs by the rushing edges of torrential streams pouring down from the cañon above in the furious storms of earlier centuries. Later the water fell away, or the river turned aside, or the hills were lifted up, and the caves were left high and dry. In due time, long after Carnack, the overhanging cliffs, further undermined by wind and rain, had cracked off and come crashing down, dislodged, no doubt, by earthquake, completely wiping out the caves. It was the scars left by these gigantic rock falls that gave Perigord his clue to their location.

At the time of Carnack we can see by the pictoliths that the Utah caves were broad and shallow, flattish, with wide, low-arched entrances, again unlike the caves of France and Spain. Carnack's caves had good roofs and dry walls; but the wide openings let in the weather. Naturally the largest caves were the deepest and gave the best protection from wind and rain, making them most desirable, which undoubtedly led to more or less strife amongst Carnack's contemporaries, for we find the biggest men, according to Carnack, ensconced as a rule in the biggest caves.

This consideration was not so important at that time and place, however, as it was in the same period in Europe, the experts tell us, for the climate was not severe. They had snow in winter; there is a picture of what is undoubtedly a mountain blizzard. Two men are shown struggling home through it. We do not know who they are. One of them resembles Blozzip. The snow is coming down and they are up to their knees in the drifts, leaning against the wind. But the cruel, relentless temperatures of European glacial conditions were absent.

The summers were pleasantly warm; not so hot as the desert summers of the present. Water was fairly abundant. We find Carnack fishing in streams; and somewhere there was a lake of fresh water. We know that it was fresh, and not one of those saline sinks found now in that region, because Carnack shows his father, hunting, coming upon a moose drinking at its margin.

The exact site of this lake has been in dispute. I have placed it as shown on the map, in the Valley of The Caves and not far from Blish's rock, because the location has geological warrant and for the following reasons: I am convinced that this was Carnack's father's last hunt. Although he appears in fragments found in the detritus which are assignable only to periods early in Carnack's life and antedating this one showing him surprising a moose at the lake, he does not appear in any that can be definitely ascribed to a later period. The fact that the actual scene of his destruction by the moose is not shown indicates nothing. All of the scenes of this period were on the loose, scattered pieces recovered from the debris and talus underneath the cliff. Some of them must have been wholly lost or disintegrated in twenty-five thousand years; it was only by luck that this much was found bearing on this particular episode.

Another fragment shows men bringing the father back to the cave where Carnack was born and lived with his brothers and sisters and Moox, his mother, until, as a young man, the events reported in this volume took him elsewhere. If the lake had been at a great distance from the cave they would not have brought the body home; for respect for the dead had not developed into a technique which required much fuss and feathers over burial. A worn-out spear laid to hand and a club, perhaps, resting across the corpse in easy reach, no doubt satisfied the sepulchral sentiments and superstitions of Carnack's people. But there is no other point near by where, geologically speaking, a lake could have been. . . . It is not of the first importance, however.

This part of Utah is, as I have said, treeless in the extreme at the present time. One lonely, crackled cottonwood struggled on at the foot of the cañon in which we came upon the pictoliths, indicating, no doubt, a feeble seepage from the spring we found in The Haunt a mile above; and several small trees —another withered cottonwood or two, three or four elders, and a tree I took to be a cedar—were disposed about the little spot where the tiny gulch with its spring came down into The Haunt.

In Carnack's time he shows us that trees, and even forests of them, were to be found in these mountainous hills; species which a botanical friend of mine tells me are at least related, as nearly as he can judge from Carnack's rough sketches, to species now in the wooded mountains of Utah, Nevada and California; conifers, oaks, ash, cedars, beeches, cottonwoods, and apparently an aspen.

The boys and I, upon our first visit, came upon a petrified tree like the one to which a by-way has been built in Yellowstone Park—but without a fence around it—still standing in the gorge at the head of the valley above The Haunt. We were working out way up this gulch to see whether it led out onto the upper ridges—which it did—when we came upon the stony old fellow, with a few fallen flinty limbs about him, clinging to the toe of the ridge serenely indifferent to his last long loneliness and the silly years that kept streaming past on silent, solitary feet. Carnack, no doubt, had rested in the shade of that tree, with Loof, his dog, more than once!

Hunting, of course, with fishing, was the chief end and means of existence. Aside from the few nuts and berries edible at certain seasons of the year and some nourishing roots and succulent plant-tips, like modern salad growing wild, and a few water plants, their food supply ranged the woods or scampered over the plains or swam in the streams, and they had to go and take it every day or starve.

Every day is, I suppose, an exaggeration. Meat would keep, for them, until it was gone. This is simple conjecture. Carnack does not show it in the pictoliths. It is not pleasant to think of him and his mother Moox and Starga and little Laa'aa tearing flesh from bone long after a Board of Health would have demanded other disposal of it; but no doubt

they did. They were accustomed to sights and
sounds and scents and savors that would go hard
with us today; and they had no sanitary experts to
tell them when their food should disagree with
them.

They ate their food raw in Carnack's time. I
stand, I am afraid, alone in this. Cassell, Fischer,
Perigord, and others lacking the opportunity to be
informed which these specialists enjoyed, insist that
the prehistoric Utah cave dwellers already had the
use of fire, knowledge of which, they show us, is
ancient and almost universal amongst savages.
Charcoal signs of fire like those in the French and
Spanish caves and the great camping ground of
Solutré were found on these caves sites. Burnt
bones were uncovered by Fischer. And so forth.

Carnack, they point out, was too thoroughgoing
a reporter not to have celebrated such an event as
the introduction of fire if it had occurred in his
time. A picture of him chipping flints, with a puff
of flame and smoke coming from a little pile of
leaves or dried spear-shaft shavings between his
knees, which I hold to be this very record of discovery, the scientists assure us is nothing more than
a description of the manner of procuring fire common at the time, or, at best, an account of the dis-

covery of a new method, the almost universal practice amongst savages being to produce it by the friction of two sticks; while the circumstance that up to a certain point fire does not appear in Carnack's records and then suddenly does, they attribute to exigencies in the narrative. He had not mentioned fire before because he had not had previous occasion to speak of it.

This view of the scientists I felt compelled to accept until a prolonged and deeper study of the pictoliths uncovered clues to me that convinced me they were wrong—amazingly wrong. I will mention only one, a picture found well over in the pictoliths, but before the point where fire itself in familiar use is first encountered. A group of men —the same group—is shown twice in obvious series, with a volcano in each scene. Amongst the men we recognize Old Huckar and Young Blozzip; Skihack, also, Carnack's oldest brother. With the first group we see a young girl. In the second group, otherwise identical, we do not find her. The volcano spouting fire behind them explains to me the absence of the maiden from the second picture. We still have the same thing amongst modern savages; in fact, we have precisely the same sacrifice of ourselves and others, although in more subtle and

insidious forms, to the things we fear amongst ourselves.

No doubt Carnack witnessed such a scene as a
boy—as much of it as a boy would be allowed to see,
at least. The fanatical and ecstatic departure of
the party from The Caves, with shouting and dancing and beating on the hollow log one of them is
seen to be carrying, the women cowering about the
mouths of the caves, children hiding away, the
mother of the victim looking on, the victim herself,
frozen with terror and despair, dumb, staring,
going straight before her; the ferocious return without her, hours later—days, I am inclined to think,
if Perigord was right in identifying Grash-po-
Nash, the volcano, as a distant crater, now extinct,
which we used to see in the next basin—with the
fervor gone, like drink died out, leaving the brute
thing they had done shouting at them. For "thou
shalt not kill," like all morality, is not an arbitrary,
trumped-up rule imposed under threat by a capri-
cious, self-appointed potentate, but the very law
of being itself, against which neither the ignorant
savage nor the patriotic practitioner of wholesale
destruction may trespass without suffering the
inner mark of his transgression.

The experts set the affair aside as a plain

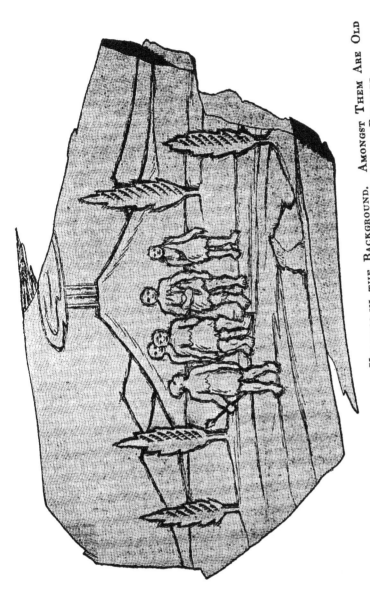

A Group of Men Is Shown, with a Volcano in the Background. Amongst Them Are Old Huckar and Young Blozzip; Skihack, Also Carnack's Oldest Brother.

religious rite. Cassell, especially, weaves the pattern of quite a religious system on this slender thread. Ingenious as it is, and appealing both to the reason and the imagination, I cannot accept it. These people, as we are to see, were too innocent, too childlike, too young in life, for anything but the most simple and direct reactions to their fear. Cassell was nearer the truth when he began than when he finished, as experts often are. The meaning of the incident and the light which it casts not only on the whole subject of fire but upon the career and experiences of Carnack himself, are too deeply embedded in the story to be gone into here at further length.

Elk abounded in the higher flats and the plains of the vast basin that lay for miles and miles beyond the foot of the hills in which these people lived. Antelope, too, were in this open country; deer in the mountains and forests and brush. Edible small animals were numerous; Carnack and his playmates could catch them. There was a large bird like the prairie chicken, sage hen, or grouse; ducks and geese, apparently, and plover. Herds of horses, as we shall have occasion to note, and bison, roamed the plains. Both were a food for the people.

Sabre Tooth, the cave tiger, who graces so many

tales, was, I regret to say, not contemporaneous with Carnack. He had been extinct in Europe for thousands of years. The large, fierce feline that he shows was a species of cat much less in ferocity and size; more likely merely the puma or mountain lion, or panther, larger than their descendants of today, but not comparable with Sabre Tooth himself. The same is true of the huge bear that we find him depicting. It was not the hideously savage cave bear, but merely a grizzly or cinnamon in the grand manner. Carnack's neighbors hunted it, and it in turn hunted Carnack's neighbors.

Judging from the pictures which, in telling us all this, bear out the collateral evidence of fossil bones found by Perigord on the site of the caves, Carnack's fellows held the great wolf of the mountains in quite as much dread as the bears and panthers. They were a fierce crew, hunting in packs, and not at all averse, probably, to a succulent citizen when he came their way, or they his, although they hunted chiefly the deer, antelope and horse, with now and then a moose or even a bison.

The record of fish and fishing is scant, in spite of evidence that Carnack himself was a skilled fisherman, apparently preferring piscatorial pursuits to hunting. Of agriculture there was none when the story starts. What weapons they had and their use of them is so much a part of the picture that will unfold in our history that knowledge of them will reveal itself from time to time in the proper place.

What their language was, its extent and character, we can only guess. Carnack certainly became able to communicate ideas to those able to receive them. For the most part their intercourse must have been objective to the last degree. Their speech probably consisted of a set of symbophones, sound symbols hardly to be dignified as words, limited to the material objects and practical experiences of every day.

On the whole, despite what seems to us intolerable hardship, barrenness and futility in their existence, they lived in their day and place as contentedly, richly and to as much purpose as we may seem to have lived in ours, to those who will follow us twenty-five thousand years hence. No doubt a race will be on earth by that time to whom the culture they will find in our social and domestic habits will be quite as great a shock as we experience when we get the picture of these earlier creatures crawling about their caves half naked, with matted hair, and raw meat in their nails, exchanging grunts and growls and gutteral gurgles and ludicrous concatenations, or forthright manual signs when impulse to communicate was strong upon them.

In one respect their civilization was higher than our own. While they were without benefit of the sixth commandment and the advantages of the teaching of peace on earth and good will towards men which we enjoy, and resorted to club, tooth and claw now and then to gain personal ends in a way that we do not openly approve today, in others, war in the large was virtually unknown. Carnack's pictoliths dispose permanently of the popular supposition that intertribal depredations and hatreds were a feature of their culture as they are of ours. Once only does he picture an event approaching war. Had there been other instances he would have told us. He was too alert and faithful an historian to have failed. There simply were none to report.

CHAPTER IV

THE EXPERTS TAKE A HAND

IT was not until I was on the ground with Perigord, the young French geologist who came over with Fischer of the Hamburg Academy, that I began to understand what the finding of the pictoliths really signified. This was on what I call the Third Expedition, although it was the first participated in by professionals.

I had not announced our discovery until we had run out to Utah in the car a second time, the boys and I, later in the summer of our first eventful visit. We were not quite ready to let others in upon our secret. I wanted to have my material in hand a little better first, and I rather think we all enjoyed a sense of exclusive possession of a discovery; although, of course, we did share it privately amongst our friends.

When we came back from our second visit I took photographs which we had obtained of the pictoliths in place and a bit of the surrounding country, including glimpses into The Haunt—we had no guess at the time as to where the caves were—and some of the engraved fragments we had found in the debris, to a friend of mine connected with the local museum, a large and important one.

He carried them to his chief who, regarding me as a newspaper man, swept them aside with the back of his hand. I wrote an article on the engravings; not too interesting because, as I have said, I had as yet no appreciation of what we had found. The head of the museum, whom I had had occasion to touch upon in my article—perhaps it was only the head of the department into which the incised stones had been dumped with such an unceremonious clatter—wrote one back completely demolishing me, and the row was on.

The magazine which had printed my first article opened up its pages to me a second time. People who could not possibly know anything whatever of the matter excepting what they knew of other matters having no bearing upon it, began to pop into print and speech all over the country. I got confidential communications from obscure individuals asking me privately the very questions I had already publicly answered twice in the magazine, tipping me a cryptic wink, so to speak, to let me know that they understood the published material was designed for popular consumption and intimating that they felt entitled, on the strength of the fellowship which their sly insight gave them, to real information; the 'inside dope', as a barber in Kansas City put it.

Then I heard seriously from Emil Fischer, of Hamburg, writing as an official of The Hamburg Academy. I answered him in kind, and he came to see me, all the way from Hamburg. I told him, with a little more detail, what I had already published; showed him my specimens and pictures; he went back to Germany, organized an expedition, returned to America, and I accompanied him, by agreement, to the field of our discovery in Utah. Perigord was with him when I joined the expedition in New York.

We spent six thrilling weeks in the Seafar Basin and its environs. An account of the explorations and discoveries of this party of scientists can be found in the brilliant and exhaustive monograph covering their work which Fischer prepared for the Academy, rather technical and dry in spots, but excellent reading for all that, available in the German upon application to the Academy; and in Perigord's report, more vibrant and human than Fischer's, although not so profound and solid, made

to the Société Anthropologique de France, now
being translated, Perigord informs me, with legiti-
mate popularizations by the author.

Perigord, who, I am inclined to think, will turn
out before he finishes to be himself more or less of
a bringer of life from the dead rocks he knocks
about amongst so much, opened up to my imagination the vertiginous chasm of antiquity which gaped
between us and the man whose personal history we
were busily reviving day by day, and stretched my
mind to comprehend, little by little, what it meant
to have come into living contact with a human being
twenty-five thousand years of age.

"Do you see that star up there, my friend?" he
said to me one night, as we sat on a little eminence
near camp in Seafar Basin after a hard, hot day
amongst the hills and gulches, pointing to one that
burned in the desert sky with flaming scintillations.
"And you know how fast light travels? Nevertheless it has taken the light from that star a million
years to come to us. It would amaze you, would it
not, if a man were to step out of that star tonight
and stand before us on this hill? Yet this fellow
that we found stalking up and down these hills today is not less amazing to us men of science," he
went on. "But that he is more so. For time that

has gone by is harder for the imagination to bridge than space which still exists. Is it not so?"

I agreed that it was.

"It is not new to us that men were in existence when this accommodating person was risking his young neck to leave a message for us on the cliffs," he proceeded. "That is not the point. Neither is it the point that you have upset all our learned calculations by discovering an unexpected people here in western America. That has happened before to us and will continue to happen to us often, let us hope. The point is that you have brought us in touch with a prehistoric man himself in his very person. Never before has this happened. Heretofore it has been possible only to see crowds, anonymous crowds, moving about together away down there in the shadows of antiquity; groups without units; formless faces without features; echoing footsteps without feet, hollow, empty voices without lips to utter them. 'Whose was the hand,' we have been obliged to ask ourselves as we turned over in our own hands the ancient specimens of cultures found in our caves in France, or stood transfixed before the astonishing parietal paintings that they have left upon their walls; 'Whose was the hand that held this implement and wrought with it in his daily life as a familiar tool? That first fashioned it from flint he found by the riverside on a summer afternoon? Whose fingers traced these lines upon the surrounding rock with a patience which we cannot even think of, my friend, and filled them in with enduring colors? Here he gripped his graving tool in tawny grasp,' we have said to ourselves. 'Here he tapped upon it with his hammer-stone. What was he like? He lived, he thought, he felt, he was himself and no one else. He looked about. He saw the stars. The rain fell on him. He would have looked around at us, over his shoulder, if we had come up behind him at his work. Our eyes would have met. What would he have said to us?'

"Hitherto we have asked all this in vain. The cultures that we have placed our fingers on in France have given us only tantalizing hints, the faintest outlines. Now this delightful friend of yours, this engaging individual, this enchanting person, this entrancing fellow over here comes marching up beside us as we pore over a handful or two of crumbled bones and broken stones that have been left behind, laboriously endeavoring to reconstruct from them a vanished race, taps us amiably upon the shoulder and resurrects the ages for us at a stroke. It is incomparable, my friend. It is stupendous. It is unheard of. It is unique. You are to be congratulated. But you are not to be surprised if some of us do not quite believe and go back to the bones to which we are better accustomed."

Perigord, however, although it was he who helped me to begin to see this man standing back there, in the murk of time, never, himself, fully fathomed Carnack or his people. He was, perhaps, more concerned, as an archæological geologist, with the fact that an individual had emerged in his own identity from prehistory than he was in the individual himself; whereas I, as an old newspaper man and a humanist, was all for the story in him. Fischer, of course, was interested in the man much as an entomologist is interested in a beetle on a pin; while Cassell, it seems to me, devoted most of his study of Carnack to trying to fit him into what he already knew about other primitives, past and present. As a consequence I am sometimes left to feel somewhat exposed and alone in my interpretation of the pictoliths on their human side—but not necessarily uncertain.

Carnack's father, I am very much afraid, was not a mighty hunter and a man of valor in his day and generation. On the contrary, I am inclined to

think that he was a bit of a ne'er-do-well amongst
them; a shilly-shallying, molly-coddlish sort of
person in a prehistoric way, bemused and ineffec-
tive; rather a soft man, in fact; although no doubt
we should have found him hard and rugged enough
if we had stumbled on his den some pleasant winter
morning while out hunting rabbits, let us say.

The best he could do for his family in the way of
a domicile, we have it from Carnack, was a small,
mean cave on the outskirts of Shoulder Hill, more
than a mile from the main community, exposed to
the full blasts of northerly storms and the first attentions of marauding beasts. Neither was his
cave-mate Moox the pattern of a woman one would
expect to find in the establishment of a man in the
habit of choosing where his fancy lit. Nor had he
more than one.

Not that Moox was not a worthy woman and a
good wife. She was industrious to a degree in
dressing animals and cleaning skins and digging
roots and gathering nuts and berries, faithful unto
death and afterward, and displayed, as we shall
see, qualities of character which would not have dis-
graced the cave of any man. But she was singularly lacking in those points of beauty which, judging from the consorts of the mighty ones—Old

Huckar, for instance, with his four fat wives—were the connubial desiderata of the times.

This estimate of the father tallies with the eventual end which has been assigned him at the hoofs and horns of a moose. No great hunter would have so far failed in skill and spirit as to have succumbed to any beast less formidable than a tiger or bear; or, at the very least, one of the fierce mountain wolves which we are to know better. And who but Blish, what hard-headed cave-man of practical affairs, who but a shiftless, trifling fellow with a large and destitute family of his own to support, would have taken in Starga and her brother Inkin when they were left by their own father to perish by themselves?

In one respect especially Moox did not fail her lord and master. She supplied him with an abundant, a redundant, progeny. I have never been able to determine how many offspring there were. I doubt whether Carnack knew. I am told he could scarcely have counted above three or four. If he could, he makes no attempt to maintain the count in the pictoliths. When occasion demands that he represent the entire family he sketches in as many as space will permit, in a long rank of receding lines, like soldiers on parade, and lets it go at that.

Some of his brothers and sisters who entered into his life in a qualitative as well as a quantitative capacity he does lift out of mere anonymous numerosity. There were Skihack and Skook and Knumf, brothers, and a sister Teltob, all older than himself, and little Laa'aa, who came after him; and one or two others introduced so infrequently and incidentally that we need not bother with names for them. When Starga appears with her younger brother Inkin Carnack is very definite about both of them. It was she whom Walter and I picked out in our first inspection of the stone slab, on the afternoon we found it.

Carnack was one of the last to arrive. Laa'aa, I think, was the youngest; about Starga's age; not quite so old, perhaps. A certain highly domestic scene to which Carnack admits us opens up a possibility that still another was born after Laa'aa. There is some confusion; the picture, which was found in the debris, is highly illegible; far beyond any hope of reproduction. It may be that Carnack is intending to represent, from subsequent observation of similar events, his own birth. If there was another after Laa'aa it did not, I am sure, survive.

Many of the family, I imagine, failed to. The point, however, is not important. It is sufficient to know that Carnack came near enough the end, if not at the very tag end, to be a little brother in a large family and to be treated accordingly, no doubt, in the rough, uncouth, uncompromising life of the cave.

Unless the picture just referred to represents Carnack's birth, we have no record of the event itself. We are warranted, however, in taking the scene as typical, and can accept it as a sufficiently faithful account of the arrival of our young life-bringer. Moox, on the musty nest at the back of the cave, leans her head and shoulders against the wall. It may be nightfall, it may be morning, it may be mid-day. It is not night, however, and the thing will not have to be groped through with in the dark this time; for Blish, the father, is skinning a deer—work Moox should be doing. The season, I think, is spring or early summer; the deer's horns would indicate that. Half a dozen other members of the family are within and without the cave. What they are about is not apparent. Whatever it is, they are paying no heed to Moox, except one female, an older daughter, perhaps, sitting doggedly by, waiting.

Carnack, in this pictolith, is not striking an attitude to show how casually such an affair was managed by his people. Why should he? How could he expect that anyone would be impressed? It is a simple matter of course that one should quietly and quite incidentally have a baby in the back end of a cave with a little assistance from someone who is not having one of her own at the moment, if that is where one happened to be when the baby came, and if someone else happened to be at hand to help.

Moox has hers, in this cave, and let us say that it is Carnack. He is ushered in, plucked clean of sticks and straws adhering to him from his mother's nest, wiped off by hand, turned this way and that, and handed over to pasture, the others continuing the while about their business, or lack of it. Blish, perhaps, looks up from his deer skinning to see whether it is another boy to help with the hunting later on. Perhaps not; possibly that does not interest him any more.

That night they throw Moox her stringer of meat from the fresh deer. She picks it up, gives it a shake, revolves it, looks it over, begins at one end to devour it, twisting her head this way and that to get at it better, curling her heavy lips out of the way, tearing off long shreds of the raw flesh with her great teeth, drawing their flapping ends into her mouth bite by bite, stopping to gulp down half masticated chunks, turning the juice to account with the back of her wrist, crooking the baby, sketchily wrapped in the hard, untrimmed, partially cured hide of a hare, in her other arm for his repast while she has hers. The noisy wrangling of the others over their food at the mouth of the cave is punctuated by the querulous gutterals of Blish and sharp squeals as he lays about him.

Dinner finished, Moox lays the little animal in the nest beside her, turns over, breathes heavily a few times, and goes to sleep. The others creep in to roost around her as darkness sets in. Skihack sleeps at the entrance to ward off prowling beasts. The stars shine down. The brook below the rock, babbling nonsense up at them, lures down their thin splinters of light to dance on its dappled surfaces. The needles in the group of pines beside the brook venture to gossip more and more in whispers with the night winds hurrying back from their daily sojourn with those other pines, silhouetted against the night along the distant lofty ridges, interlacing their branches with the stars. A twig breaks. A wolf howls. A sleepy squirrel scolds over the disturbance. Blish stirs and grunts in his sleep—

hoarse, broken syllables, low in his throat. Night murmurs run through the slumbering group; now and then a child cries and is roundly clicked for it with knee or knuckle. The stars wheel on.

In the morning Moox is up and about her affairs again, leaving Carnack in the bit of fur on the bed of musty rushes. Blish, I suspect, drifts off to the cluster of caves under Shoulder Hill a mile away. His deer of yesterday will do until he gets another one. He will loiter up and down the trampled, littered ground before the caves, employing eyes and ears upon whatever comes his way. He will linger to admire the spoils the hunters have brought in. He will stop to see one of them mend his spear, refastening the loosened spearhead to the shaft with deerthongs. He will sit apart in the sun watching another work out a club or throwing stick—scraping it down to form and smoothing it with tools of flint. He will lean against a tree while a group of three or four, grunting, clucking, chip out instruments or weapons; spearheads, scrapers, knives. He may pick up a discarded piece of flint which he can finish. Blish, as we are to know, was more expert at this than most. He will exchange a grunt or two, perhaps, with some of them. But not with Old Huckar. Old Huckar with the burning eye—the eye with the sun in it that no man dares look into.

And there he lies, little Carnack, at the back of the cave, day after day, night after night. He does not cry much. The race has been learning for ten thousand years, or a hundred thousand, that it is not well to make helpless and inviting noises in a lonely cave, and their young remember. Furthermore, why should he cry? What is there to cry about? He knows of nothing that he wants. The race knows of nothing that it wants but raw meat and shelter, of which he has a present bountiful equivalent. Now and then he squirms, letting out another link; now and then, as the weeks go by, he opens wide his eyes and mouth and emits a tiny cave shout over some amazing discovery of thumb or toe; now and then he stares with infinite intentness at some movement of the others in the cave; a fight, perhaps, over an oily bone one of them has found or a fresh quarry just brought in. Now and then Moox comes to him, squatting on the ground to take him up and feed him. Some of the others, the smaller ones, crowd around at such a time, clamoring and pushing. She sweeps them away with the back of her hand or sends them spinning with a click of her knuckles on their bare heads,

excepting the youngest, perhaps. Carnack, of
course, thinks nothing of all this, makes no note of
it, does not worry about his supply. Everything, to
his unasking eyes, is just a part of life, like everything else.

I am very much afraid that a dainty modern
mother would not care to pick the little fellow up
and nuzzle him with kisses. He is not a cute little
bundle of dimity sweetness, all pink and white and
delicately scented. His sole garment is a roll of
rabbit skins, some still stiff and some limp from
previous use. Hygenic arrangements are entirely
wanting. Of water and the bath he is serenely innocent, unless perhaps Blish takes him down now
and then on pleasant days later on to hold him
naked in the running brook to harden him.

Nights and days continue to pursue each other,
then as now, in the march of time. The grass on
the hills and beside the lake turns brown. The
leaves dry out and rattle from the trees. Cool winds
blow up the cañon. The mountain sky turns brazen.
A tang comes in the air, the brass turns into lead.
Snow flies. Winter comes. They lie huddled in
the shallow recess of the cave. The snow reaches
in to them on the midnight winds. A drift forms
across the entrance, sloping down to nothing at one

end, leaving them barely room to go out and come in. The drift keeps out some of the wind, but the top fringe of it becomes a continuous feather of whirling flakes that powder down on Carnack's face and tiny body, melting there and leaving little drops of water on him; all a part of life, like everything else. It is difficult to keep the hare skins on him. No one tries particularly. He cannot keep them on himself. Moox takes to carrying him around wrapped in her own skins, next to her bare, warm body.

Meat keeps better now—when they can get it. Blish brings in a fresh kill now and then, throwing it down for Moox to dress and divide, and slouching off to the nest with clinkles of snow and ice clinging to the hair on his legs. These melt off and trickle through the twigs and rushes and dry grass when he lies down, pulling the hairy skins around him. There is great excitement in the cave; squealing and squabbling amongst the younger ones; pushing and loud cries amongst the older. Blish has hacked off a fat piece and devoured it on the way home.

Skihack, no doubt, is custodian of the nuts they gathered in the fall. He keeps them in a chink in the rock, doling them out. They crack them on the floor with hammer-stones, throwing the shells clear of the nest. Skihack has a running fight on his hands with rats, which help themselves. He steals out of bed and across the frosty floor day and night to inspect his hoard. Woe betide the rat he lays his hands on! Then, we can be sure, there is a great clamor amongst his charming brothers and sisters, tumbling out of their furry coverings at the first squeal. We know him too well to expect that he shares it; unless Blish, perhaps, demands it for himself. They watch him in a circle, hair matted over their eyes, faces strained and pinched, bodies taut, limbs drawn, shivering with the cold, nursing icy, aching feet on aching, icy shins, the snow from the drift fringe powdering over them; slinking back to their nest again dull-eyed, twitching, clicking their teeth. Has Carnack a memory of such a scene? Though he must have witnessed many of them in later winters, he has left us to draw it for ourselves.

Skihack, too, takes to the hunt, we can assume. Skook no doubt goes with him. Knumf, perhaps, as well. They bring back rabbits, a squirrel or two, a few partridges. In the light of later knowledge I can guess that Skihack sometimes contrives to join Young Blozzip on the hunt—Blozzip the

Hairy One, brother to Sooash the newest and favorite wife of Old Huckar. On such occasions he must come back better laden with supplies, for Young Blozzip is already a great hunter and fortune favors those that go with him.

Long nights, bright days, with a snow storm now and then. Blish, I can imagine, scarcely stirs from beneath the piled-up hides for days, but lies there dozing and staring, staring and dozing. Moox and the others leave him alone. Nevertheless Moox sometimes lifts up the furs and lays Carnack down beside him, and Blish lets him remain. Carnack does not know that he is cold. How should he? The race does not know, in terms, that it is cold.

The snow dies out of the air in last fluttering flurries. The sun renews its warmth. Fantastic cliffs and jagged crags in miniature appear in snow banks, reaching up from the crests of the drifts, pointing in parallel to half past one in the sky, where the sun is hottest. Tiny, fantastic, jagged caverns strike down into the snow beside and about the pinnacles and peaks, burrowing away from the sun at its hottest. Little rivulets flow from beneath. Patches of rock appear, draped with fringes of lacy ice edging the departing snow. The bare spots grow. The drift across the mouth of the cave shrinks and shrivels in upon itself, becomes pitted, hard, soiled. Cast-off bones gnaw their way into it through brownish, loose-fitting holes. A flange of clear ice skirts it, just free from the ground. A wide, deep margin creeps across the rock about it, expanding daily. Opened areas on sunny slopes widen and merge into each other. Southern ridges are exposed throughout their lengths. The brooks boil and tumble between ragged sheets of crumbling ice. The white patches on the summits retreat into the cañons, withdraw to sheltered corners, steal into nooks. The rough, sandy soil, soft and oozy, crunches once more under foot. The chill leaves the air at noon; morning and evening mists appear; the days grow longer. Soft-cheeked breezes come welling up the cañons, float across the ridges. Green peeps out here and there. A bird comes; a flower or two. The cave men emerge from their caves, clubs and spears and hammerstones in their hands, grunting in the warm sun, squatting with their backs against the sun-warmed rocks, tinkering their implements. Cave women venture a hail or two from rock to rock. Children swarm down into the mud to explore the world once more. The ceaseless strained rigidity in neck and back, the numb pain in muscle and limb, the aching stiffness in feet and hands, relax and disappear. The men take up their clubs and rehabilitated spears and push out upon the plain where the game has taken winter refuge and remained unmolested during the deep snows, to make the hunt. They hear the boys shouting in the woods of the brook bottom as they go by. Some loiter at the lake to look for ducks. Some fish. Blish searches out a warmer rock to lean his back against while he chips his flints. Skihack and Skook make the hunt this year in earnest. He will follow in a day or two. When it gets a little warmer.

CHAPTER V

LIFE AS HE FOUND IT

THE records of Carnack's infancy and childhood are necessarily scant. Walter, in the spare moments of our first brief stay, cruised diligently up and down the loose, rocky slide where the cañon wall had been rattling down for two hundred centuries, and we combed its scaly sides exhaustively on our second visit, but we have only a few scattered fragments picked up in the debris beneath the cliff to guide us; fractured, chipped, spalled off, some quite illegible, others unintelligible, with nothing about any of them but their content to determine order, period or relationship.

How much there may have been originally we shall probably never know. Attempts to search the talus more conclusively on later expeditions proved ineffectual. Fischer had no funds to divert to sentimental explorations into a problematical cave artist's past, and Perigord had other fish to fry. Cassell did lend us a laborer with pick and shovel for a day or two on the Fourth Expedition, but the fellow had no imagination or desire and un-covered nothing. You must love such things to find them. He merely dug. The thought still haunts us of much rich material that may still be lying deep beneath the surface at the foot of that soli-tary, far-off cliff-side.

When the experts were appealed to for help in filling in these early vacancies with guesswork based on their knowledge of other primitives and modern savages they only plunged themselves into hopeless disagreements. Perigord and Fischer especially were at tremendous odds about every possible detail of domestic life and practice in Car-nack's times, making the velvet curtains of the desert night tremble more than once with their dis-cussions of the probable scenes and circumstances in which a child would have grown up amongst these dwellers in the caves. Cassell, on the other hand, was merely erudite and dull.

Later on I came to see the radical mistake in turning to modern barbarous tribes for a com-parison with original peoples such as these. A study of the pictoliths themselves, which reveal a prehistoric race as nothing else has ever done, con-vinces me that the analogue between true primitives and so-called savages is not a sound one. The

parallel runs much more evenly between the savage
we have with us and the highly civilized people of
today, carrying steadily, under a mask of changing
idiom and gesture, through religious institutions,
commercial customs, superstitious morals and the
social order. For modern savagery is not a first
state, not a dawning culture, not an initial or an
intermediate step in a long march toward civilization as we use the term, but a finished product within and withof itself, a completed culture, a con-
cluded record of long ages of self-education in its
peculiar fears, reactions and credulities, a civilization of its own achieved and rounded out, with nothing more ahead of it, outside of revolutionary individual regeneration, but to wear deeper into its
long-determined grooves. Somewhere back beyond
forgotten time mankind as we now see it stood at
the parting of the ways. Some chose the path that
led to the jungle and the hunt; the dart, the arrow
and the boomerang; the fetish and the voodoo;
head-hunting, human sacrifice, and unbelievable,
trumped-up gods they all came to believe in. Some,
that which led to the factory and farm; the tene-
ment, the town house and the bank; the submarine,
the aeroplane and poison gas; serums, vitamines
and psycho-analysis; the social register, cigarettes

and jazz; the incense pot, ecclesiasticism, and all
the modern gods of self and fear and greed and
personality. The people that we see in Carnack's
pictures are still at the dim parting of the ways.
They are beginners in life's racial journey, ignorant
and innocent, having as yet learned neither to be
good nor to do evil, as unlike the modern savage,
described as "half devil and half child", as the child
who pulls the cat's tail because he does not know it
hurts is unlike the child who pulls it because he
knows it does.

How would a miscellaneous group of such a
people, herding together in a cramped and crowded
cave, lorded over by the strong man and chief
hunter amongst them; hairy, heavy-footed, putty-
shouldered, thick-eyed, mirthless; guided by instinct and impulse alone, unswayed by reason, un-
checked by any law or sense of law outside or in but
the law of the strong—how would such a group
regard and treat another of their kind thrust in
amongst them helpless and unasked for? Would
he be only one more mouth to keep filled up until
the time came when he could turn around and help
to fill up theirs? Would there be any sentiment of
tenderness or interest among them beyond his

mother's instinct to protect and preserve him for a little while?

I think not. I imagine that the brothers and sisters of the particular little animal that we left lying on a brush heap at the back end of a cave twenty-five milleniums ago paid about as much attention to him, from Skihack down, as they did to any of the other things in life about them—the sun, limbs of trees, loose rocks, ants going in and out—and about as little. When he was in their way they put him out of it with foot or knee or open hand. When he was out of it he was out of their thoughts, like everything else in their lives.

Moox, we can be certain, went to him at intervals in the early days, when pressure prompted her or he made known his wants, picking him up and putting him down again on the brush bed, keeping an eye out in the intervals between for rats that had escaped Skihack, and snakes, driving off the other young, even cleaning him, conceivably, now and then, with her great hand, forever unwashed, or a hank of rabbit skin. Later on she hands him meat to suck and chew on and brings him fresh, wet bones to cut his teeth on. Then Laa'aa comes. . . . Blish, I have always fancied, was good to him from the first, sitting and looking at him.

When the first spring comes round he without doubt is taken out on top of the great rock that stood before the cave—and still stands, although the cave is long since gone. This rock, located by Perigord on the Third Expedition, and identified by flints found on the site showing the fine workmanship singular to Blish and to Carnack later, was a harder burl of the mother cliff worked down into the form of a huge half-boulder by the very waters that at the same time were gouging out the cave. When the waters went away they left this rounded, dome-shaped rock with the cave perched at its crest; and its flattish, uneven top, which was really an extension of the floor of the cave, now served the family as abbatoir, front veranda, back yard, playground for the younger children, tannery and disposal station, and, in pleasant weather, as dining-room, general boudoir, living-room and sleeping-porch.

Blish, or some previous occupant—more likely that—had scooped out a flight of shallow steps or niches up the side of the rock where it butted in against the mother cliff on the up-river side, toward Shoulder Hill, and another flight, even cruder, in the angle of the opposite junction. Or perhaps countless feet through countless centuries had worn

them in. Besides these there was no other access
to the rock. Its smooth, round sides were otherwise insurmontable; which, with a tangled thicket
Carnack shows us fringing its base, made it a capital
formation for defence against wolves or bears or
mountain lions or, as Fischer suggests, other cave
men looking for apartments; although Blish's
quarters must have been singularly exempt from
that form of intrusion, in any case.

Here, on the rough, uneven, broken surface of
this rock, full of illogical sudden slants which must
often have precipitated offspring, implements,
spearstaves, clubs and what not into the impene-
trable thicket below, Carnack is let down, on a day
when the sun has begun again to start the sap of
life within the cave, to burgeon in the warm lap of
the season and be under the maternal eye. And
here, naked and unafraid, in the midst of an inviting miscellany of small bones weathered white,
scraps of fur, shreds of skin, fractured flints, discarded hammerstones and splintered spearshafts
strewn about the top of it, he begins his education.
The leathery, angular Moox, with skins thrown off
a little in the warmth to give her freer movement,
kneels on the rocky ground engaged upon some
pelts that have accumulated from the winter's hunt-

ing. Softer weather has thawed them out so that she can work them now. She scratches and picks off the shreds of fat and putrid meat with her huge nails, or pulls at the tougher ones with her teeth, scrapes the insides of the hides with blades of flint which Blish has cunningly chipped into sharp, even edges, beats and kneeds them with smooth, heavy stones, breaking their stiffness. Occasionally she stops to study the one in hand.

Blish, let us hope, is off to the hunt at last. Skihack and Skook, with Knumf, perhaps, are undoubtedly out in the hills. Teltob, with the surge of spring in her veins, has stolen away to the cluster of caves under Shoulder Hill. Blozzip, The Hairy One, ready now to mate, does not look at her; but there are others about. She strolls past, thick-lipped, heavy-eyed, smouldering, pretending, perhaps, to hunt for cresses along the margin of the brook that goes about its business within eyeshot of the caves; although everyone knows that the outlet of the lake far below is a better place for that. Or perhaps not. Perhaps her wooing is more forthright and frank than that.

The anonymous ones, the score or more of brothers and sisters, are ranging the broad, flat floor of the valley. Some of them have gone to the lake to splash and catch a turtle or two, and frogs. Others have treed a squirrel and are flinging impotent rocks and sticks at it in the top of a pine, where it sits jerking its tail and scolding at them. Some mingle with the children from the caves, tumbling and pushing and chasing each other.

Carnack does not miss them. He is too much engrossed in affairs of his own on top of the rock. He has found the skull of a rat; one of Skihack's rats. He does not know what a rat is, or what a skull is, but he does know that the thing he has found is excitingly hard and smooth and white and shiny, and has funny sharp things in it, and a part that moves up and down, until it comes off, and holes he can stick his fingers into, and get them caught in. He waves his arms and shouts about it, and when he looks again the thing is bouncing off across the rock. He starts after it, naked knees on abrasive floor, but comes upon a clinky, gleaming flint on the way, or a shred of hairy skin, or some bug setting up housekeeping in a crack, and forgets about the other.

So his education starts, and so proceeds. If the others contribute to it at all it is only by clicks of the knuckle on his stiff-haired head when he gets in the way or pursues a line of conduct which, if per-

sisted in, would break one of the simple safeguards
against the dangers of cave life that these people
have worked out from grim experience. In the
midst of the most engaging explorations of the
cave or the steps leading down from the front yard
to where the others go he finds himself suddenly
clicked and brought back dangling by an arm. He
is clicked in the height of experiments of the last
importance with funny things that crawl about the
rock, or come buzzing up to it, or with shiny black
things that Blish, The Other One, keeps doing
funny things to. If he tries to help The Other One
with the funny little black things he gets solemnly
clicked for it. If he goes off about his business as
likely as not The Other One throws pieces of the
shiny things after him and makes him come back;
then clicks him. It is all very confusing.

Skihack, a hunter in his own right now, no
doubt takes a responsible hand in the clicking.
Skook and Knumf head him off and herd him in.
Teltob shoves him heavily aside with her great
bony feet, clicking him adroitly with her toes. The
seasons of her wooings probably go especially hard
with him. The anonymous ones swarm over him,
knock him flat, take things away from him. But
nobody tells him why; nobody tells him what it is

all about; nobody tells him anything. No one replies by so much as a look to the great wide eyes
opening on life. How can they? What is there to
tell him? What do they know themselves about it
all? Then Laa'aa comes.

In due time he learns to walk. He has to, to get
what he wants; the others stop bringing him things.
Blish keeps creeping into this event, in spite of all
I can do. We have a picture which may be a direct
account of it; a splinter found in the talus, in which
the little man, always so bemused, is standing beside a pool of water at the creek with an infant in
his arms, a tot of one or two. Fischer, character-
istically, puts quite a different and sinister construc-
tion on the scene, but the proportions of Blish's
family alone are enough to prove him wrong.

We have no means, of course, of knowing that
the babe is Carnack, but we are fairly safe in assuming that the picture is not of anyone else, and that
Blish, on some warm, idle summer afternoon, let us
say, when Moox is off hunting roots and berries
with Laa'aa on her back and no one else is about
the cave, has taken him under his arm and stolen
away with him to the creekside; the first of all his
offspring, we have reasons for believing, to be so
singled out.

Blish goes to a spot he knows beside a pale, pebbled pool with a willow and elders draping about it, where he deposits Carnack on the crunching stones and pliant sand at the edge of the water and squats against a tumbled log in the embrace of rustling mountain grasses. A blackberry bush nods over his shoulder. A fish darts away and steals back again. A bird stops singing, but recommences soon.

Blish throws off his strip of summer fur, caught about his flanks with a flint pin. He picks a berry or two from the swaying blackberry spray and eats them; an incommensurate champ for his swinging jaws and tough yellow teeth.

Carnack sits in the sand among the colored stones. Blish goes into the water. His slight body, hollow-chested, heavily haired over breast and shoulders, down spine and arms, on thighs and shins, moves through the pool in a series of quick jerks. The cave men have learned how to swim; Carnack shows us this more than once, in his pictoliths.

Blish takes a few strokes, the limit of the pool. Carnack, very busy, continues with his own affairs. Blish comes out; drips off; lies on the warm sand; gets up; goes in again; comes ashore; picks up Car-

nack; wades out with him; immerses him once or twice; floats him atop the pool, Carnack objecting at first.

They come ashore. Blish squats against the log in the dry sunlight. He picks up a flake of bright red rock. He holds it out to Carnack. Carnack starts over for it, along the ground as usual. Blish stands him on his feet, holds out the piece of rock again, stands him on his feet once more, clicking him when he throws himself down for locomotion; teaches him to take a step, and another. Teaches him to walk.

I do not know, of course. All this is sheerest fancy. It might have been this way. Or it might have been some day on top of the rock, or some twilight evening, perhaps, when the others were away short distances, Blish making a lure of a bit of shiny flint he had been working up, or a bone, or a hank of fur. But I like to think that it was the way we have pictured it. And I like to think of Blish stealing home from the pool furtively in the late afternoon with Carnack under his arm jabbering a cave syllable or two, perhaps. It is time, or nearly so.

Does Blish smile as he bears him home unnoticed? Did he smile over the first faltering steps at

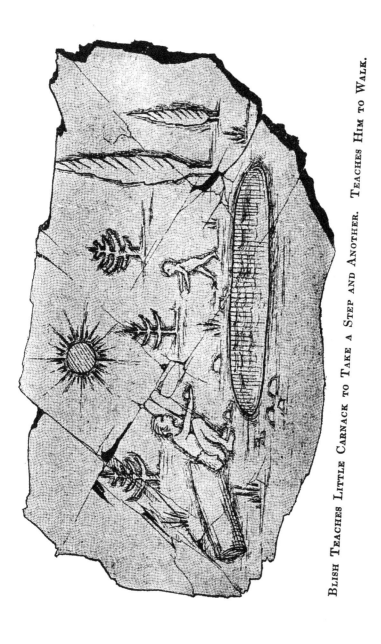

BLISH TEACHES LITTLE CARNACK TO TAKE A STEP AND ANOTHER. TEACHES HIM TO WALK.

the pool-side? Does Carnack learn to smile? Do
these cave men know how to smile? They laugh,
we may be sure—laugh over the ludicrous misfor-
tunes of their mates, with mighty roarings; laugh
in glee over their own safety in the face of danger
that distresses others; laugh at their own successes;
laugh at the kill, no doubt; at the lucky stroke of
club or spear; laugh, perhaps, although I doubt it,
at the antics of their young. But the smile, I am
satisfied, has not yet broken out upon the human
countenance in parted lips and dawning eyelight.
For the smile is too much of the spirit. Although
Starga smiled.

Carnack, of course, could have had no memory
of such an episode of his infancy. Blish must have
told him about it later, in reminiscent mood. More
hangs on this than at first appears. It proves communication, between these two, at least, of abstract
ideas. It is evidence of a companionship between
them which was unique and without a counterpart
amongst Carnack's people until Starga awoke to
him, and he to her. His youthful comradeship with
Heetow was superficial and objective; it did not
reach beneath the surface in their thoughts about
themselves, or each other. The apparent friendship between Skihack and Blozzip was a practical

habit of convenience and mutual material advantage. They got along together well in hunting and in hiving. While Inkin's devotion to his sturdy-legged brother of the cave was merely planetary.

But above all, this second-hand and reminiscent picture of his infancy shows us that Carnack was self-conscious. The ego had been lifted up in him to see and recognize itself. He meant something to himself that interested him in events involving him that were not present at the time. He had picked up the thread, however clumsily in his blunt mental fingers, of continuing identity. His recognition of a past implied a perception, however vague, of a future. When he learned about the episode and when he put it down upon the rock he was aware, although he had no memory of it, that he had been that very babe; saw that from the first he had been himself and no one else, and would remain so when he was as old as Blish, as old as Old Huckar. Not before had this happened. Not before had man looked beyond the immediate generic impulse to maintain the individual and perpetuate the species. His light had come and flamed within him and he stood on pinnacles of time, alone, the first, surveying promised lands of consciousness.

Chapter VI

He Takes a Look about Him

WE do not get another glimpse of Carnack in the pictoliths until we come to a fragment in which we find him, a toddler of four or five, standing on the summit of the family rock looking out with eager interest upon something from which his brothers and sisters apparently are scurrying out of sight, like frightened rabbits, into the recesses of the cave.

It could be a prowling wolf that is putting them to flight. There were plenty of them thereabouts. But I do not think it was. A wolf would no doubt have frightened Carnack also. I have quite a different version of the scene. I do not wish to be understood as insisting on it, but I have fancied more than once, from what we learn later about this Carnack, standing erect and beginning to think, that Old Huckar, or Young Blozzip, or some other mighty tribesman from the caves, may be passing by at the time along the trail that threads down the

mountain valley not far from Boulder Rock, on his
way to the lake, or to hunt in the basin below, or
to cross the lower ridges into the next cañon for
deer or bear. The other children scamper off at
sight of him, but Carnack stands his ground. They
try to drag him with them, but he sees no reason
for it. Why should he run? What is there to run
from?

I can see Old Huckar, trotting by in the ambling
shuffle which his huge, short, crooked legs and
squat, massive frame imposed upon him, turn his
head quickly and fix Carnack with the fiery eye, the
eye with the sun in it which no man could look upon,
as he catches sight of him. He stops in his tracks,
perhaps, to fling an intimidating gesture at this
son of Blish the Woman-Hearted, naked and upright on the rock, gazing at him.

Perhaps—I am far from urging this—perhaps
Old Huckar, or Young Blozzip, if it be he, is
stirred into a vague uneasiness, a faint, far-off fore-
boding, at the sight of a little boy that does not run
away but stands and looks. He does not know, nor
can Carnack, nor do we, many of us, of the final
threat, the fatal danger, the certain promise of
annihilation to false authority and prestige based
on egotistic personality or mere force which lies,

not in bold-faced challenge that can be met with
boldness, but in eyes like these that gaze upon im-
posture calm and unafraid, in guileless innocence
which the imposter cannot cope with because he
cannot understand it. He does not know this; but
the blind, frightened, self-preserving instinct we
have spoken of, as sensitive to its dangers as a
hunted animal, may easily sense this one and
prompt Old Huckar to a fumbling, silly threat in
turn. "For the weapons of our warfare are not
carnal, but mighty through God to the pulling
down of strongholds", and the strongholds know it.

Moox, no doubt, rescues Carnack from his temer-
ity with prehensile arm, sweeping it out upon him
from as much concealment as she can contrive and
still reach him, whisking him out of sight and
roundly clicking him for—what? She knows no
more than he. Or perhaps this correction is reserved
for the moment when Old Huckar—or Young
Blozzip—shall have vanished into the distance and
the silence and the brothers and sisters, late ecstatic
victims of their own created panic, come swarming
forth to vent their sense of outrage and vindicate
themselves upon the one who ignores the proprieties
and will not be afraid.

Carnack, when he came to write it in the records,

must have had some sense of the significance of the stand he had made that day upon the rock. He must have seen when his whole world was beginning to close in upon him because of other questions he had asked of it and answers he had given back, and he stood before his lonely slab on the distant cañon's wall uttering his story to the insensible rock, that this was the first prophetic footstep in the path in which he was being led, the first outplay of that unaccountable and perverse spirit in him which, whether or no, was setting him farther and farther apart from the others in the Valley of the Caves. Otherwise he would scarcely have gone to the trouble of including the incident in the records, for in itself it was insignificant enough.

What he was really doing was etching an idea that had etched itself upon his consciousness. It was not the only idea that he drew. We find him doing it in many instances. Therein is at once the wonder and the peculiar treasure of these records, and their most amazing difference from other prehistoric drawings known to man. More than all else about him this gift of fumbling through to the idea distinguishes him as a seer amongst seers and an intelligence of the very highest order; for it is in relation to their own times that men emerge, as my young friend said in his theme about the will of God.

This original man had no precedent to carry on, no tradition to refer to, no known tool to his hand or scrap of ascertained material with which to build. He had only himself to work with; himself and that Mind which there was no one to tell him about or instruct him in but the Mind itself. Yet he made advances and took steps and created a life for himself which, judged by the criteria of his times, is one of the outstanding achievements of all times and makes the awakening and illumination of this first known thinker of the race a covenant of inspiration between the Source itself of all intelligence and every man. Carnack, lifting up his wistful face down there in the dusky pit of time, pulling himself out of the clay that he was digged from, is a symbol and a promise of man supreme in his own right above his circumstance.

We have this same double value of objective and subjective record hinted at, although a little more obscurely, perhaps, in another scene that we come to in the fragments recovered from the talus. It is a clear cut and well preserved pictolith of about the time of the incident on the boulder. It might be earlier, it might be later. There is some contention over it. I have placed it later. The point is of no importance.

It shows Carnack standing face to face with another boy of about his own size and age. They are staring at each other with that forthright curiosity and unflinching frank appraisal which only boys can compass.

Of the other's identity there can be no doubt. His nose, or lack of it, proclaims him to be the one we shall call Heetow, Carnack's boyhood chum, youthful companion and sometime hunting partner. The picture was undoubtedly drawn to celebrate their first encounter; but was it drawn for more than that? Is it a hint, and the first one, of the many directions in which Carnack turned, in innocent good faith, before he saw the chasm that yawned between him and his fellows and objective life about him, for that contact and communion with reality which was satisfied at last, as he believed, in the friendship of the wolf that came to him? I, at least, so construe it.

Whether this first meeting takes place at Carnack's rock with Heetow in the rôle of unexpected visitor or whether Carnack, engaging in a journey of adventure and discovery, has wandered for the first time into the precincts of the caves at Shoulder

Hill where Heetow, son of Palupe of the three wives and one of the mighty hunters, resides, we are not told; but his audacious and defiant curiosity toward life supports the supposition that Carnack was far more likely to have been the initiator of the incident.

Not far from the foot of Boulder Rock, Carnack shows us, where the cave of Blish stood, a cluster of pines lifted their conical green crests on tawny, slender stems upright from the flat valley floor. Between their parallel upstanding boles and through the lacy geometric silhouette of their branches a blue glimpse of the lake beyond peeped up at those upon the rock—and peeped in vain for the most part, I imagine.

Whether it was the peaceful and provoking beauty of these pines, with their inviting open vistas and soft, smooth, saffron ground between that might have lured him off the rock, or a sheer spirit of exploration and romance, I will not pretend to say, but I can see the young Carnack early launching expeditions to them; first a laborious, crab-like, all-four backing down the long, steep steps in the angle of the rock, at great expenditure of patellar and phalangeal epidermis, attaining possibly within a few feet of the bottom before interruption falls upon him with female cries and clicks; later a more expert and expeditious clambering, back first to be sure, though with freer legs and arms, but still unsuccessful, family vigilance having kept pace with his developing technique in ambulation; then a neatly picked, fairly swift sidewise climbing with only now and then a steadying assistance from the hands, which may have brought him to the ground and well on his way, only to be borne back ignominiously by Blish or Skihack or even Skook with much clicking and guttural injunction. For it is one thing to go thronging through known groves and thickets and across frequented valley floors in a noisy, clamorous crowd of youngsters, and quite another to steal away quietly by one's foolish little self and wander invitingly into the jaws of who knows what wolf slinking about for just such an opportunity, or the maw of a panther balancing hunger and discretion on the margin of the settlement.

But the day comes at last. The father and the bigger brothers are off hunting in the hills. The lesser brothers and the sisters have trooped away in berrying groups, the boys hunting eggs, perhaps, with an eye out for squirrels or a baby rabbit. Moox, we may guess, is deep in the cave stirring up the family nest—adding new material, as she sometimes has to do. Teltob is no longer with them. One night, as the sun was going down, she had come running toward the cave, hair flying behind her, skin garment flapping over her up-thrusting knees, teeth gleaming, eyes half closed and misty, with a young man, who was not Blozzip, in pursuit. We have such a picture. I have not fixed the time. Perhaps it belongs before the episode of Huckar's passing by. It really does not matter. The young man, overhauling her at the base of the rock, clenches his fingers in her flying hair and pulls her back from the first step of her ascent.

It is here that the pictolith catches the scene. Moox, it is not hard to guess, is laughing—something we rarely find her doing. Blish, squatting at the base of the cave's proscenium arch, does not disturb himself, apparently. Skihack peers over the edge of the rock, watching; Skook and Knumf look on over Skihack's elbows. The man, whirling Teltob about by the hair, proceeds to make off with her in round, reluctant goose-steps. She is, we can imagine, making a suitable to-do. Carnack looks around, sees no one doing anything about it, picks up a bone and flings it after the man. For which unquestionably Moox clicks him well. Skihack, likewise, and the others. Especially, perhaps, Blish. Without permanent effect upon him, however, for it is not the last time we find him intervening, with the same unaccountable internal prompting, but with more discernment, in support of the rights of others to themselves and their own devices.

So Telbob is not there; and the tell-tale attentions of little Laa'aa, tagging him about on top of the rock, Carnack has silenced no doubt with a ruthless and fraternal click as he slips over the edge and begins his scramble down the rough steps.

He reaches the ground and gains the cluster of pines undetected. Their tops are a-twitter with birds, flitting about in the branches, making the needles tremble and leap. He can hear them snapping at the cones to get the seeds out. He knows what they are. Skihack and the others bring them in to the cave to eat. They flutter and cheep all day long in and out of the thicket at the base of the rock. He has had a peep into their nests from above; has seen their eggs that no one can get at to suck. He may have had a roll or two off the rock in amongst them. Who knows?

Squirrels are hurrying back and forth in the tree tops. He knows about them, too. Skihack and the others throw sticks at them. Occasionally one

CARNACK OVERTAKES THE GIRL, TELTOB, AT THE BASE OF THE
ROCK, CLENCHES HER HAIR AND PULLS HER BACK.

comes tumbling down. The pine branches are tossing them to and fro. Sometimes one of them runs
off and sits on its tail and shouts at him. Then
they all begin. He throws sticks to make them
stop. The missiles do not reach half way up, and
the squirrels only shout the harder. There is a
breeze up there; it blows the ends of squirrels' tails
and flutters the needles.

The air tastes good. The ground is softer than
the rock at home; softer than the bed he sleeps in.
Excepting that it prickles. He finds sticks honey-
combed by worms, and pine cones, some of them
stripped by the squirrels.

He walks up and down, touching the trees, keeping an eye on the cave; ploughs into the needles
with his naked toes; gazes down through the lofty
colonnades about him to the lake shimmering in the
sun; considers pushing on to it; discovers the trail
passing through the pine cluster; looks up and
down it, wondering where it goes, where the people
come from that he watches from the rock, going
up and down it; wonders, perhaps, who they are,
what they are like.

Someone is coming up the trail now from that
vast, mysterious unknown region which he has seen
from the cave, stretching out and away down past

the lake illimitably to where the rocky jaws of the returning mountains crunch down upon its farthest edge.

He hides behind a tree. He does not want to be interrupted. He does not want to have anything happen to his being alone, to his doing whatever he thinks or does.

But something does happen. We have the identical picture of the calamity that descends upon him in a fragment, defaced and half obliterated, but still decipherable enough to permit one to trace out Young Blozzip and what seems beyond a doubt to have been intended for Skihack. Some lines in the background, very faint, characteristic of Carnack's habitual representation of the pine cluster, locate the episode. Blozzip, we can see, has something in his hand that might well be a slaughtered squirrel. He and Skihack are quarreling over it.

It is easy enough to see what has happened. Skihack and Blozzip, returning from their hunt empty-handed, unless some uintelligible lines, badly erased, at the bottom of the fragment indicate a deer that they have bagged, discover Carnack, whose skill at concealment is not enough to serve him against two keen-eyed, quick-eared, sharp-scented hunters.

Skihack throws a stick at him. He cannot wait to lay hands on him. Carnack starts to run. Skihack throws another stick at him. Carnack has to dodge it. The next moment Skihack has him by the shoulder.

A squirrel in the tree-tops begins to scold at the commotion. Skihack, without releasing Carnack, throws a stick at it. Blozzip unlimbers a short, smooth club which he carries for the purpose and hurls it at the squirrel, which dances about in the branches and shouts at them louder than ever. Finally it comes tumbling down; one of them has hit it. It falls at Carnack's feet. He picks it up, soft and warm, still jerking.

Blozzip clicks him on the head so hard that he knocks him over, picking up the little animal as Carnack drops it. Skihack comes up quickly, not to succor Carnack but to claim the quarry. He lays hold on it. Blozzip clicks him. Skihack clicks back, with a stick. Blozzip leaps upon him, sinking his teeth into Shihack's shoulder. He aims at the throat, but Skihack saves himself from that. They go down in a tussle, Carnack looking on. There is grunting and growling.

Presently Skihack subsides. Carnack, picking up the squirrel, makes off with it. Blozzip goes back and picks up his deer, if it is a deer, and strides off towards Shoulder Hill. Skihack, scrambling to his feet, nabs Carnack again and drags him off to the cave, clicking him at every other step.

But there comes another day. Once more Carnack is amongst the pines before the cave. A year has elapsed, it would seem, if we can rely, as we often must, upon the fidelity of Carnack's scale, for the boy in this picture is a size larger than he was in the last.

He watches the birds and the squirrels for a busy moment, shies a futile stick or two at them, circles the stems of the trees, keeping well out of sight of the cave, finds a beetle or two and eats them, picks up a sound bit of branch broken off from a tree, whacks the trees with it, whacks the ground with it, comes to the trail that runs through the cluster, beaten hard and smooth like places on the rock where soil has accumulated and been trampled down by the family's bare feet, looks this way and that along it, strikes out upon it up toward Shoulder Hill. He will find out where the men come from that he has seen going up and down there. He will learn what they are like.

He whacks with his stick as he goes; grass, plants,

bushes, trees. He trots a few steps and falls into a walk, whacking with his stick. He emerges from the cluster and finds himself out in an open grassy place with which the view from the rock has made him familiar; sees the rock with the cave atop it; sees Moox; breaks into a run, as tight as he can go, bracing himself against screeches of discovery from Moox, determined to go through with it and not be deterred by a voice.

Ahead of him a flow of hill comes down onto the level valley floor, spilling trees ahead of it. The trail curls in behind it and disappears. He reaches the shelter that it offers and drops into a walk. Moox cannot see him here, screech as hard as she will.

The path, swinging off once more, dips through a growth of elders and willows, skirting the stream, shallow and smooth and purling here. The narrow, winding footway, soft and spongy, cool and moist, with here and there a stone or a root-knuckle bulging up, is gracious to the little fellow's feet, toughened though they are from long acquaintanceship with the hot, rough, rocky floors at home.

A fish darts out of sight into the deep green lobe of a pool at the top of the shallows. He steals over and peers in; sees nothing; whacks the pool; comes back.

Birds rise with sudden chirrup from the thickets and dodge away in undulating flight; swift flutter of wings to climb the ascending arc; arc of descent with wings tight against the body; sudden grasp of the air again at the bottom of the downward sweep, and upward swing once more, over and over again, each swing bearing them forward.

He proceeds upstream toward Shoulder Hill, loitering, taking his time, poking into bushes for birds' nests, plunging after frogs at the water's edge.

Presently his ears, pretrained by hundreds of centuries of racial existence in the open, catch the faint fall of feet in the trail behind. He slips into the brush, insinuating himself without a sound and without a trace into the dense growth. He has learned better how to hide from clicks and interruptions.

His two brown eyes flash from the depths of interlacing green and grey of leaf and bough. In due time they catch broken glimpses of two men winding along the margin of the creek. They are carrying something on a spear shaft slung between them. We have the scene on a recovered pictolith.

One of them is Young Blozzip, the Hairy One. Carnack can see the cloud of hair upon him; the dark, springy, glossy coils on thorax and shoulder, thigh and forearm, nape and spine, that give us his name. He is huge; but not so huge as Huckar.

The one who is with him in Skihack. The thing they are carrying is part of a young horse. The spear is thrust through the animal's body, leaving the smeared ends free for each to bear on his shoulder. As they draw abreast Carnack can see the knots on the bare pole of the shaft, worn shiny by the grip of Blozzip, underneath the juices of the horse's flesh that stain it now from the flint spearhead, set into its split end and made fast with deer thongs, all draggled now, to the butt.

A low gutteral escapes from Blozzip's throat. They stop. Carnack with the stick he picked up amongst the pines could reach out and touch the massive back of the Hairy One. What if he should?

They set down their burden in the cool shade; prodigious burden for two men to stagger under all the many miles out of the hot basin, where the horse is found, up through the steep, scorching gorge, across the valley floor. Blozzip scoops up water for his thirst. Skihack kneels to drink.

Blozzip, tossing the spilled drops out of his beard, sniffs and glances around, with a grunt of query and defiance. Carnack sinks softly to the ground and squats there.

Skihack answers Blozzip with a gurgling clack. They exchange a grunt or two, satisfy themselves, pick up their piece of carcass, and resume their way to Blozzip's cave. Carnack, emerging from his concealment with many listening pauses and glances up and down when their footsteps die away, follows after them.

The trail, leaving the creek, crosses another open grassy space toward a grove of oaks that overflows a low, broad, rolling ridge. Behind them a tawny, high-shouldered hill lifts up its head. Clumps of bushes dot the open place. Carnack explores amongst them, circles around them, looping back often to the trail. He does not hurry. Moox must have missed him by this time, but she cannot see him now. If she follows he can easily avoid her.

He reaches the edge of the grove and enters it.

He begins to hear a sound, indistinct, muffled by distance.

He cannot get hold of it.

Then he makes out the murmur of voices, far off,

difficult to fix, punctuated by lulls, and his heart turns over in him.

These are the men he sees going by! This is where they come from!

He presses forward; no diversions now.

The sound grows continually more distinct.

Presently he catches glimpses through the trees of a red cliff ahead.

Then, suddenly, through spreading trunk, branch and leaf, beyond a grassy tilt of land that runs down from the cliff to the brook, he sees, in the bright face of it, caves—caves like his at home, only bigger.

He quickens his pace to a trot.

The voices rise to a steady hum, with now and then a shout or howl or a roar or screech breaking up through. He hears women and children.

He whacks a tree and falls back into a walk, all eyes and ears.

As he comes closer he sees movement in the caves —sees someone stand up, take two steps, squat down again. He sees others arise and move around; men he has never noticed before. Old Huckar he knows, Blozzip he knows; but not these. He stops and looks around, his stick resting on the ground.

The path widens and splits off into branches that

embroider the ground. Other caves come into view; still larger ones, crowning the gentle, oak-strewn eminence that slopes down from them to the creek. The ground in front of them is beaten solid and smooth; littered with debris; bones, skins, skulls, broken spears, pieces of flint, old discarded clubs.

He sees men sitting about in groups or alone. Their booming gutterals and rumbling growls dissolve into syllables that he hears at home. The squeals of children, spattered with the shouts of boys, streak the air and echo to him from the base of the towering cliff.

He sees women, sometimes two or three together, squatting on the ground at cave entrances or bending over hide or carcass of the kill; hears them talking. In one of the largest caves he sees, or thinks he sees, Blozzip and Skihack cutting up the horse. Groups of children flow about in streaming, chittering bands, like the flocks of birds he sees in the open place in front of Shoulder Rock when the grass gets brown, before the white stuff comes. He feels unaccountably comfortable, unaccountably lighthearted and cheerful, unaccountably safe and relieved, unaccountably glad.

Thus his meeting with Heetow, as I have liked to fancy it, in the very height and heat and hunger of his discovery of the surprising world and all the people in it. A scurrying group of youngsters skimming past, perhaps, and this one detached by circumstance or drawn aside by curiosity, or something more, at sight of Carnack; a glimpse caught by Heetow from his cave in the cliff of a strange boy, a slow descent, a measured approach, one cautious, fully planted and built-up step at a time, a set-to and a tussle, it may be, or long silences and furtive beginnings, a breaking down of reserves and building up of understanding and ease; a chance collision, rounding some tree, as Heetow comes on the run to overtake his mates, or escape them. A loitering together, taking care to avoid Skihack. A test or two of strength. A display of caves to Carnack, and of Carnack to the children of the caves.

Then the walk home, teeming with discovery, through the late afternoon, along the strange new path full of mysterious shadows now and disturbing noises. Back to the solitary cave, with no one in it but The Big One and The Other One and Skihack and the rest.

And Little Laa'aa. I can see him hunting Little Laa'aa out in a corner of the dusky cave that night, after the clickings which receive him home, with a piece of horseflesh in his fist which Skihack has doled out to him begrudgingly at last; squatting down beside her; eating it slowly, giving Laa'aa little pieces of it that come loose.

The cluster of pines with the birds and squirrels in them is a silent, reminiscent silhouette against a rosy sky, the mountains toward the setting sun a bank of lavender filled with purple shadows, the lake, a widespread brimming bowl of ruddy wine.

And up at the caves . . .

Chapter VII

He Sees a Number of Things

IT is not until Starga appears six years later, as nearly as I can estimate the interval, that we get another view of Carnack in the fragments from his early life. No doubt the cultivation of the boyish friendship of which we have just witnessed the inception led to much sturdy trudging back and forth along the trail from Boulder Rock to Shoulder Hill and Shoulder Hill to Boulder Rock in these six years; clandestine at first, we may assume, enjoying by slow degrees a tacit sufferance which at last settled into a fixed acceptance of a fact accomplished. We can be sure there were excursions to the lake as time went on, explorations of the valley, expeditions into the surrounding hills. Unquestionably the gorge below the lake came to know the echo of their voices; more than once their eyes must have looked out into the basin which it led to, stretching its taut, hollow plain, like a gigantic hide pegged out to dry, to a far-off horizon of dim, distant mountains; and it is not impossible

129

that they may have pushed across intervening ridges and through intercepting cañons to a first view of the little mountain shelf behind the waterfall of which Carnack was to see so much and which we have come to call The Haunt. But we have not a scratch on stone to show for this. What adventures overtook them, what dangers they endured, what hardships they subdued, what hunts they went on, what animals they met, what fish they caught and how they caught them, we can only guess.

I for one would like to know what our young lifebringer was like at this stage of his existence. On some points, of course, we can be only too certain. Never by any chance, it must be remembered, did this lad, or any part of him, undergo a washing, except accidentally and incidentally in fishing or in scooping up a drink from the creek, or in plunges in the lake or river pools. His head was beyond question a tangled mass of matted hair hanging over his eyes, full of dried grass, crumbled leaves, bits of twigs, clots of dust and no doubt worse. His teeth were white, if they were white at all, by virtue of sand and grit mixed in with his meat or adhering to bones he gnawed on. His ears were forever innocent of maternal solicitude, his nose knew no handkerchief at any time, his nails were blue, jagged crescents at his finger tips, his feet thicksoled and horny, with perpetual, accumulated stains between his widespread toes. In winter his body was wrapped, or partly so, in harsh, foul skins with the hair on them, discarded only when cracked or torn beyond further usefulness or no longer needed for protection from the weather. In summer he was as naked as the desert day. Always, I am afraid, he swarmed with vermin of the season; gnats and flies, fleas and mosquitoes, ticks and jiggers, and what not.

Manners he had none. Life in the cave, as well as out of it, was rough. Attention to the comforts, wishes, feelings of another was beyond the mental grasp or moral instincts of the family group. Food was always the first consideration with each one. The appearance of meat was a signal for a scramble; a squirming knot of hungry animals hovering over the fresh kill; while every sundown saw a scuffle for the warmest, or the softest, or the safest, place in the nest. When game was scarce, or the season too severe, the weakest, and especially the old, went under with scarcely a glance from the others; although the very young, if sound, were cared for by the mother instinct, which would hardly let offspring perish from avoidable neglect. Blish,

I imagine, came first in everything in the early days. Skihack later challenged this, I think.

So we may picture Carnack at this time dirty, unkempt, circling about the outskirts of the family group, grabbing for any food that came his way or was going another's, making a foray now and then upon the center of supplies and getting clicked for it, or not, as the others have had enough or not. We can see him, bare arms extending from beneath the scant skins he wore, devouring his rations in a corner and stealing off to bed when he is through to forestall the others.. We can see him, when the weather comes on colder, poking about in heaps of skins lying here and there in the cave and on the rock for the best one he can find; pulling it out; trying it on; watching over his shoulder for Skihack or Skook the while. See him making himself scarce; keeping out of the way; practicing only enough assertion of himself to keep himself alive and not enough to bring the others down upon him.

Did this young Carnack, who saw on every side of him, in the daily round of life, animals ferociously slain, flayed, quartered and eaten out of hand, and the remnants tossed aside to must in fetid heaps; who saw men and women and the young taking what they wanted from each other if

they could and could not get it any other way; saw
disputes at home and amongst the people in the
caves at Shoulder Hill settled with fist and club and
tooth and claw, rarely to the end, to be sure, or
more severely than was necessary to gain the point,
but decisively; saw no thought expressed in voice of
gesture or behavior that did not have directly and
exclusively to do with keeping the belly full, the
skin whole and the body warm or otherwise ap-
peased—did he take it all for granted at this time?
Living in the midst of such squalor and confusion,
such filth, turmoil and unfettered instinct, did he
accept it without question as a part of life? Or was
he beginning to have a first faint surmise that this
was not all; that this need not be as it was; that
there was something different and better possible?

Was he like the other boys of the settlement;
rough, savage, boastful little beasts, looking forward only to becoming mighty hunters like the men,
or did he sometimes steal away from their fierce and
boisterous maraudings to listen to the song of birds,
whether edible or not, when spring was come and
he felt the stir of something else within him?

Did he, in passing, stop now and then to linger
where some flower nodded at him from the grasses
in the early summer breeze? Did he loiter by the

way to watch the squirrels scampering in the tree-
tops, or ducks paddling on the lake or wheeling
down the evening sky, or did he want only stir-
ringly to kill and eat them, as the others did?

Was a deer in the woods, a horse on the plain, a
thing to him of grace and beauty and exciting freedom, or only so much potential food and clothing?
Did he like to lie unseen beneath a tree in summer
fields, a jointed stalk of grass between his teeth,
arm under head, leg over knee, gazing through the
leafy screen at the interminable blue of the quiet
sky or the white clouds piling up behind the mountain rim? Did he sometimes leave Heetow and his
mates, the cave people and the caves, to climb the
pinnacle of Shoulder Hill or the cliff behind The
Boulder and hide there while the sun went down
in lonely splendor behind the far-off ridges to the
westward?

Did he, when he could, and the sky was clear,
linger unobserved outside the cave while the others,
at the first touch of darkness, crept off to sleep,
to watch the slow swing of the stars through the
soft, grey pools above, or the drifting sparkle of a
firefly here and there, or the far-off flare of Grash-
po-Nash? Did he listen in deep, soothing peace to
the silken hushes of the night; its teeming silences?

Did he thrill with something far from fear at the sleepy breaking of a twig in the bushes, the swish past of a bat, the downy beat of an owl's wing, the ululations of the wolf-pack, remote, aloof?

Did such nights hover softly over this young lad, with his face alift in them, peopling themselves with whispers he was yet to learn the meaning of; brooding premonitions of thoughts promised but still unformed, nameless, vague? Did he dream in such an hour of something better than a bigger cave to live in with four fat wives, like Old Huckar? Something more satisfying than mighty killings and a belly full?

Or was he as uncouth and violent and heedless a young animal as any of them, squealing and fighting as ferociously, throwing sticks and stones as brutally, robbing birds' nests of the last egg and drinking down the spoil as ruthlessly, slaughtering rabbits and squirrels as savagely and eating them with as much gusto as the best of them?

I do not think he was. What later brought him out from amongst them and made him separate had, I think, begun at this time to lay its touch upon his arm and beckon him aside.

We have signs that something was already awakening within him. M. Perigord, nosing about the site where he had located the community of caves under Shoulder Hill, turned up, one afternoon, a random stone which, when he examined it, proved to have lines and scratches upon it placed there by a human hand. There could be no doubt about it. Intention rather than accident was perfectly clear in the markings, crude and inconclusive as they were.

Perigord correctly assigns them to the attempt of some artist dwelling in the rocks to represent familiar objects. But he does not accept them as necessarily Carnack's. Here we disagree. There were no other artists of the period amongst these people, or of any other period. Had there been we would have found other traces of them. But no carvings of any kind excepting those we know to be Carnack's have been discovered in the region. This stone is beyond question a crude experiment in pictoliths by Carnack himself, a first rude effort of the boyish hand, made under a prophetic impulse in an idle moment, to limn life about him as he saw it then.

This view of the solitary specimen from Shoulder Hill is supported and sustained by similar examples, unmistakably of Carnack's work, found under Blish's cave, and some sketches, the authorship of which, although developed and refined in the same hand; reveal, in fact, the very stages of the development itself.

The picture, as may be seen from the reproduction of it—the original is in the possession of M. Perigord, to whom I am indebted for the excellent facsimile from which the illustration is taken—has no value in itself but it is priceless in the glimpse it gives us, which Perigord would render dubious, of our young life-bringer as a child already scribbling in the rocks; and a proof that it affords thus early of the love for his people and the life at The Caves which was a motivating passion with the one who, in due course, would have brought them life more abundantly had they been ready to receive it.

For the presence of this drawing, near the caves at Shoulder Hill, makes it plain, I think, that the young Carnack spent much time in the vicinity. The community, I am convinced, became his favorite and familiar spot. Since the afternoon of his first encounter with Heetow in their precincts, every day, broadly speaking, had found him early in the oaks at the foot of the cliff and upon the beaten ground before it or loitering about the caves themselves, drinking in the life there, thrilling to its stir and accent, turning hither to the people, I have come to think, for the first appeasement of the hunger for a larger life which was, in the end, to drive him from them.

He watches the hunters departing in pairs or in groups, on springy stride, spears and clubs in hand, through the dappled shadows of the oaks, a ringing note in the few short syllables they interchange; follows them with observant wistful gaze as they vanish in the distance or amongst the trees or around the foot of a hill, these bound for deer in the higher ridges, those striking across into the opposite slopes, that group setting out on a hunt in the basin that may last for several days—or weeks—before they come stalking back again on slow, firm feet, with their burdens on their shoulders—hides, flesh.

He listens for the last faint, far-off sounds of their retreating voices long after the familiar routes have swallowed them, wondering what adventures they will have, eager for their return to see what luck. He turns to the caves, watching the women, hearing them cackle and cluck over the beginning of another day with their men gone. He watches boys of assorted sizes foregathering for their various affairs; sees clusters of girls setting out with scraps of skin to bring home berries in, and fruits

and tender slips; nuts, if it is fall. He exchanges a
salute with some older boy who notices him. He
picks up and examines cast-off flints, hefts broken
spear shafts, lifts old clubs and swings them.

He has faced Old Huckar more than once, we
may imagine, and found nothing from which to run
away. Old Huckar sometimes grunts at him as
he jogs past on his way to the hunt or meets him in
the trails, but more often he does not, I surmise.
Young Blozzip knows him, no doubt, as one of
Skihack's brothers. Skihack lives with his one wife
in a dark and noisome corner of Blozzip's ample
cave. Carnack does not go near the place. Why
should he? Skihack has done nothing but click him
all his life. Teltob and he have forgotten their
relationship. It means nothing to either. They
know each other when they meet about the caves,
but nothing more than that. Teltob is following
in her mother's wake. Half a dozen babies hang
about her in the loops of the skins she is dressed
in, or underfoot.

He hunts up Heetow, we may guess, when the
hubbub has subsided, and they undertake an expedition of their own, getting back in time, if they can,
to be there when the men come in. They have
junior clubs and spears· and javelins picked up,

made over, cut down by themselves, or worked out from original material in sketchy boyish fashion. No one pays any attention to them. None of the hunters help or hinder. The elaborate practices of instruction and initiation, such as we see in modern savages, are lacking. Boys must learn for themselves.

These boys learn, of course; learn to find their way; learn to strike out across the hills, dip down into rugged cañons, pick their way through underbrush, and come out where they want to be; learn to steal noiselessly and unseen up to spots—open places, little glades, tree clusters—where they may expect game; learn to cast the javelin and thrust the spear and hurl the throwing stick. Now and then, perhaps, they bring home a deer or antelope, or pieces of one, dragged between them; staggering into camp with a mighty pride amidst the shouting of the men that are back and the squealing of the other boys that swarm and swing about them when they appear.

Then, in the setting sun, we see him trudging reluctantly along the path from Shoulder Hill to Boulder Rock, bringing back his contribution to the family store—having himself first eaten heartily and made sure. But it is not this, it is not Heetow, it is not the hunt and the kill, it is not the men themselves that hold and excite him. It is the life and the promise of it that all these many people, expressing life, still hold for him.

Carnack had been having about six years of this when Starga came. Her appearance in the midst of Carnack's sisters and brothers, abruptly, with a younger boy who turned out to be Inkin, her brother, adding two more for the bewildered Blish to keep filled up, was a complete surprise and puzzle to us when we came to it in the pictoliths. We had no clue as to who she was, where she came from, or how she got there. No previous pictolith contained a hint of her. Then, suddenly, on a fragment we picked up, she was there amongst them. That was all we knew.

She seems at first to have been, as nearly as modern society can supply an analogue, half guest, half adopted sister, the guest merging by degrees into the sister. Carnack apparently accepted her on that basis, and continued to. We see him with her and Laa'aa, who was, as has been stated, about of an age with her, several times in some of the pictoliths of this period that have come down to us in the debris beneath the cliff. Once they are down by the creek, apparently, once, on a hillside; once, paddling in a dugout on the lake. On one occasion Heetow is of the group; on another little Inkin tags along. At another time Blish is with them; a rather amazing fourth for the times, I have often thought. If these pictures are important I have failed so far to come at the meaning of them.

Walter and Oliver solved the puzzle of Starga and Inkin. After the larger pieces of the splintered pictured rock had been recovered from the sloping sides of the talus, they began to pick up fragments—especially on our second expedition—of the crumbling waste, some of them no larger than a thumb nail, which they took home with them as a joint possession. It became a form of amusement with them, odd times, when other interests lagged, to fit these fragments together and reconstruct Carnack's twenty-five thousand year old picture puzzles; a fascinating form of entertainment when the difficulties of having no pattern to go by, of not knowing how many pictures there were supposed to be or to what picture any given fragment might belong, of frequent unintelligibility of the fragments themselves, and of often lacking half a dozen key pieces in one picture, did not make the undertaking too tenuous and tedious.

In this way, after more than a year of recurrent

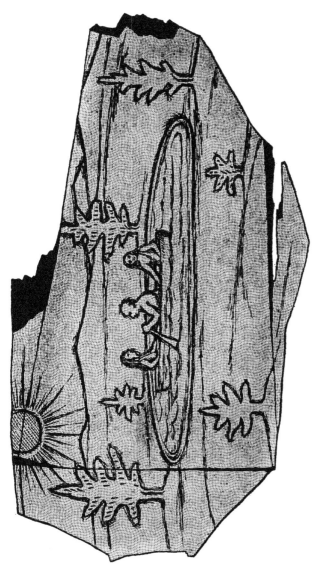

The Boy, Carnack, Is Pictured, with the Girls, Starga and Laa'aa, Paddling in a Dugout on the Lake.

attacks upon their fragments, they pieced together with really remarkable success a number of scenes which would otherwise have been lost to us. Among these was one that, despite segments missing, quite unmistakably showed a man being set upon by a pack of wolves, and another, even more fragmentary, representing a young girl and younger boy sitting alone at the mouth of an abandoned cave.

From these two taken in relation to each other, which forms a foundation no flimsier than others upon which we are compelled more than once to rest corners of this structure, we can build up Starga's story. It is she, with her brother, who is sitting at the mouth of the cave, waiting for someone to return. Who should it be that they were waiting for but their father, and where should he be, if not gone a-hunting? But why their attitude of anxious waiting? The absence of a father at that time upon a hunting expedition left a cave as unconcerned and tranquil as a modern apartment with the father away at the office. Clearly, this father is overdue. And why is he overdue? What is detaining him? Obviously, the wolves have consumed him in the other picture. So he will never come back.

But why are they shown with such dreary emphasis to be alone, these two, with no one else about the cave? Because they are alone; no brothers, no sisters, no mother, and now no father. The mother has died in giving birth to the brother, or to a succeeding child that did not survive its mother's experience with it; birth, no doubt, in spite of Carnack's casual report of it, being a bit too difficult at times even for them, on the rough rock floor of a draughty cave with no hot water at hand. Otherwise we know there would have been more children.

By the same token, we know there were no other wives. So the children were, to use a modern term for it, orphans in full. Which meant starvation for two so young. They would slowly and quietly die. No man would lend a hand habitually. No one would come to the cave day after day with food. No organized society stood by with charitable institutions for them to disappear into. We know from what other pictures reveal to us of these times that the old, the sick, the unable, the helpless young, perished softly, at one side, as a matter of natural course; just as blighted berries cut off from the nourishing sap of the bush sink down through the twigs to lie in the grass and rot with no stir amongst the berries that remain.

But Blish, passing by in the nick of time, finds them so and takes them home. Blish the ne'er-do-

FRAGMENTS OF A PICTOLITH PIECED TOGETHER UNMISTAKABLY SHOW A MAN BEING SET UPON BY A PACK OF WOLVES.

well, Blish the happy-go-lucky, Blish the improvi-
dent, father of hungry hordes; maker of excellent
flints which he did not know what to do with.

Who but Blish? Skihack, who would not have
performed the charity in any case, has long since left
the parental den and set up cavern-keeping for himself in his corner of Blozzip's cave. Skook, as in-
capable as Skihack of the rescue, has likewise flown
the nest. Knumf seems to have disappeared, which
is one of the unsolved mysteries of this history, as,
unless I am incredibly mistaken in later identifica-
tions, he shows up again later on. The others, the
anonymous ones, are not to be considered. Which
leaves only Blish.

Unless, perhaps. . . . There is one other possibility. I can see Carnack wandering by alone, or with
Heetow. The cave is, like Blish's in the outskirts,
on the farther side of the cave cluster at Shoulder
Hill. I can see him stop, hearing a cry; a wail from
Inkin, it may be. Carnack approaches. Heetow
warns; lions wail like that. Carnack reaches the
cave. He sees the two crouching there, frightened
and afraid. He takes in the situation. They have
been going over old bones, he can see. Starga has
found a nest or two of eggs; fresh shells lie about.
She has brought in some berries. Carnack encour-

ages them to come with him. Heetow protests. He
is alarmed. Carnack herds Inkin on ahead of him.
Starga brings up the rear. Now and then they stop
to rest. They make a detour around the caves at
Shoulder Hill, where Heetow leaves them. They
reach the Rock and climb it. Moox stares. The
others circle slowly about. Blish howls, accepts the
event and enforces it upon the others with cuffs and
kicks right and left amongst them, newcomers as
well as the old ones. Laa'aa, perhaps, shares her
meat with Starga. Carnack throws Inkin a piece of
flesh, where he sits out of the way still frightened
and afraid. Blish sees to it, when the time comes,
that they have a place in the nest.

While the wolves sniff about the abandoned cave
up beyond Shoulder Hill.

It is barely possible.

CHAPTER VIII

HE BEGINS LIFE ON HIS OWN

CARNACK, as nearly as I can make out, was a lad of fourteen or fifteen when they brought his father home from his ultimate encounter with the moose on the borders of the nearby lake. A stripling of about that age, marked with the beginnings of Carnack's distinctive calves, appears in the scene showing the return with the body, and again in a picture recovered from the talus of what Cassell and Perigord assure me is a funeral feast— a group of men gathered together in a cave, meaner even than Blish's, devouring an animal, while the guest, or host, of the occasion, who had been put to it all his life to find enough to devour, lies apart under some skins with his feet protruding.

The significance of the protruding feet has been and still is in dispute. Whether the skins covering the bier merely happened to be too short for the purpose and Carnack was too literal in his description of the last rites to make them long enough, or whether there was some superstitious and symbolic

meaning in leaving the feet free is an open question
which everyone is at liberty to answer to his own
satisfaction; as, indeed, he may feel free to solve
any of the problems which the pictoliths present.
Perigord advances an ingenious theory, which
others take more seriously than he does, involving
the decedent's social status; Cassell, something
about his impending journey. For my part, the
point seems of the thinnest possible importance, and
purely academic.

What did the young lad think when they
brought his father home from his last hunt; the last
of his unremitting efforts to find food? What ran
through his mind when the others laid their burden
down and he looked upon the silent, grey, broken
thing that had so lately been going in and out,
walking up and down, gazing at him?

Did he have a new comprehension of the one who
now lay without response before him on the rocky
floor of the mean cave; who had so often cuffed and
kicked and pelted him with stones, no doubt? Did
he understand better now the querulous impatience
of the man, hunted by hunger, with Moox, indifferent dresser of skins, forever bringing him more
mouths to fill, and all about him the mighty hunters
bearing home spoils in plenty; Old Huckar, with

his four fat wives; Young Blozzip, already with two
and walking up and down in front of Huckar's
cave; his own Skihack, mingling with the great
ones? Had he groped through to the smothering
sense of ineffectiveness and futility in his father, to
which the little man must forever give the lie at
home by knocking them about?

Had there been between these two a dumb, fumbling recognition of something common to them
both which left a blank and trembling emptiness in
the one now that the other was gone? A dull consciousness together of a bewildered restlessness and
query smouldering in the heart of Blish which was
to leap into clear-burning flame in Carnack? A
mutual prophetic instinct that the father's futility
and failure were but a challenge against life in the
caves which was to ring out again triumphantly in
the son's audacious successes? Blish, the apparently worthless and ne'er-do-well; Carnack, the
priceless achiever. Blish, the seemingly leaden and
dull; Carnack, the golden and glowing. Blish, the
shiftless incompetent; Carnack, the doer, the getter,
the builder. Blish, the resourceless; Carnack, de-
viser of arrows, bringer of fire, tamer of animals.
Blish, the indolent chipper of flints useless to him
and to others; Carnack, the maker and trader of

better ones, original merchant, inventor of business, father of industry.

Had the younger felt the hunger and the yearning in the heart of the older which, in himself, was to become the drive and magnificent impulse that should wrest destiny his way, make his life the glorious adventure under God which it proved to be and fling him, before he was done, far outside The Valley of The Caves where Blish had repined, to die at last under the hoofs of a moose? Had he tried to answer it? Did he reach out now, in pity and bereavement, for what was gone and unfulfilled between them?

Or did he only think, in sudden panic and dismay, of the load that had lurched into his unsupported hands within the hour? That now he himself must go out and find and overcome the wild things of forest and plain, thicket and hill, cañon and mountain side? What did he know about circumventing those wary creatures that had habitually baffled and eluded this old hunter? How could he sway them with his stripling strength when this muscled man had been slain by one of them, and that not a ferocious one? Yet he must, or they would die. Skihack was gone. Skook was gone. Knumf was away on his long and mysterious sojourn in other parts. No man would lend a hand. No other hunter would absorb the mother and her brood.

We do not find the answer to our question in the pictoliths. The interval between the arrival of Starga with her brother at the cave and the going out of Blish is a barren one, so far as pictures are concerned. We have the fragments showing Carnack with Starga and Laa'aa down by the creek, up on the hillside, paddling on the lake, in which we catch a glimpse of Blish. There are a few splinters of home life, apparently. One fairly good picture shows Carnack fishing from a rock, with Inkin standing by; Carnack's spear poised in the very act of plunging into the water. In another he is hunting with Heetow; pursuing a deer which eludes them at first by leaping a rock, but does not escape them, I imagine, or Carnack would not have gone to the trouble of mentioning it. No doubt there was a companion picture which describes the kill; their first deer, we may suppose. A fragment, badly mutilated, reveals a boy that might have been Carnack following a man who certainly was Blish, the man carrying a javelin or spear, the boy evidently a hare or some other small animal that they have bagged. Another, quite complete and well-preserved, pictures Blish and Carnack standing side by side looking off at Grash-po-Nash, smoking, and no doubt muttering, in the distance. Possibly this contains a hint. Perhaps Blish is here inducting Carnack into what there was of tribal lore. But there are no other clues to a companionship between them.

Excepting, of course, that delightful pictolith, remarkably undamaged and decipherable, which shows Blish instructing Carnack in the art of working flints, one department of cave life in which this man was a sure and contented master.

I can see them now; Blish, expert that he is, squatting on the ground with Carnack, all eyes, beside him, knocking off the grosser portions with firm, swift taps of a hammer-stone, delivered with minute precision, bringing out the form of the spearhead, knife or scraping tool that he is working on, later chipping it down ever finer and finer with pressure applied steadily at opposite points of tiny flakes he wants now to remove until they let go with faint chicking clinks and the rough contours and jagged surface are reduced to more delicate mold and texture; graceful, smooth, so excellently fine that Fischer and others, veteran experts, examining specimens found twenty-five thousand years later

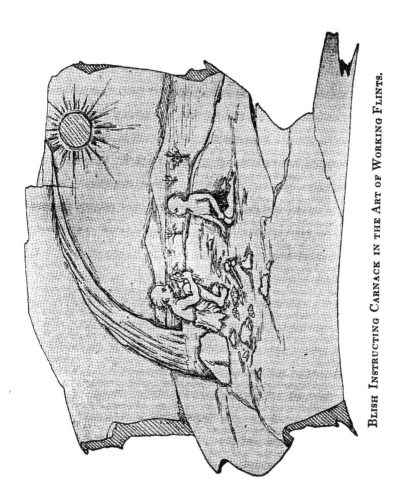

BLISH INSTRUCTING CARNACK IN THE ART OF WORKING FLINTS.

around Boulder Rock, pronounced them amongst the most perfect they had ever seen.

Now Carnack tries his feebler and unpracticed hand, whacking ineffectually upon the nodule or piece of one that Blish supplies him with, failing to make fractures at all; splitting off too much; not enough. Wilful planes of cleavage set themselves up in spite of all that he can do and run away with him, going off at tangents, returning, twisting, until at last the implement originally aimed at comes out curved and all awry, whittled down to half its intended size, lumpy, lopsided; Carnack the while, no doubt, suffering more than one click from the lean knuckles of Blish for his awkwardness. Or did Blish only grin at him? In time, however, the pupil far outstrips the master, as we learn from flints of Carnack found here and there about The Haunt.

This is all the light we have. If Carnack tried to write on the rocks the story of a dawning human love between his father and himself, the attempt has crumbled into dust.

It would be charming if we could say that the hour of his extremity, when he stood with his two boyish hands pitted against the wild beasts of field and forest which he must now kill that the others and himself might live, witnessed the discovery of the bow and arrow.

It would be pleasant to celebrate prodigious deeds of skill achieved by this young David with a hitherto unheard-of weapon that killed swiftly and from afar, to the amazement and terror of Old Huckar and Young Blozzip and the other mighty hunters who would have left them all to starve.

But it cannot be so reported. The two little pictoliths from which the invention of the bow is derived show too old a Carnack for that, and are found too far over on the rock. So he had to face life as it presented itself to him with no advantages but his two hands and his wits.

We have a picture of him of about this time standing in the oaks before the caves at Shoulder Hill with a spear in his hand; a large one, that might have been his father's.

We cannot know, of course; but I can see him marching off thither in a day or two, when the meat at home has given out, to the people at the caves.

He still feels the joy and the urge of them, all of them, herds of them, living together, close in their dens under the red rock. He feels their security; feels their support.

Skihack, we are safe in assuming, has not come

near the parental cave since the event so freighted with change for it. Skook, perhaps, has stopped by for a moment on his way to The Basin or the lower ridges, or on his way back, to heave a strip of meat onto the rock.

Whether the two came down from Shoulder Hill to celebrate in feasting the obsequies of the succumbent to a moose who rarely had enough to eat · himself, I cannot say. They are unidentifiable in the pictolith of the scene.

Carnack, in any case, is not intending to resort to them. Or to Huckar, or Blozzip, or Heetow, or to anyone. The idea of assisting one another, excepting as it had broken in on Blish in the case of Starga and her brother, has not yet dawned upon the race at Shoulder Hill. Carnack simply wishes to be with them. Perhaps he hopes to join himself with some of the older hunters. He may be looking for Heetow. They have hunted together before.

He reaches the oaks and stands on the smooth, hard ground beneath the hill.

He has just met Old Huckar in the trail amongst the thickets, swarming down the path in the swift, shambling gait that could carry him so far.

Carnack, stepping aside to allow him to pass,

had looked at him expectantly, a little hopefully, as the old fellow charged by.

Old Huckar, trotting straight ahead, had swung his piercing eyes upon the lad for an instant, then swung them off again into the distance, ranging far, from lifelong habit, for prospective food.

Carnack had taken a few paces after him, tentatively; but Old Huckar, half wheeling around, had sent him off with a grunt and a growl and a gesture.

Carnack had proceeded toward the caves, trailing the end of his father's spear on the ground.

Now he stands amongst the oaks, looking through them to the caves.

Most of the hunters have left.

A few with full stores from yesterday's hunting remain behind to mend their spears, tone up their spear points, work out new shafts, cut a new club, or idle in the sun.

One or two pairs, late in getting off, are still on the bare, beaten ground before the cliff.

Two are debating which direction to take.

Two others are giving their weapons a final overhauling. One of them is not satisfied with the head of his. It is not fastened on firmly enough to the shaft to suit him.

His hunting partner, impatient to be off, is snarling at him. They are both growing angry.

A third group of four or five, aiming for the basin, has just finished gathering itself together and puts itself in motion as Carnack comes up.

He starts over towards them, but stops and stands still, watching them out of sight.

The women cackle and skreel.

The two hunters who could not agree settle their differences about the road to take and take it.

The other two, running short of words, fall to blows and go off peaceably together in another direction.

The women subside.

Bevies of youngsters stream by into the woods and fields.

The men remaining at home move about the entrance to their caves, under trees; squat down with their work, jabbering and gesticulating at each other over it in the intervals between crucial operations.

Carnack approaches the caves; strolls in front of them.

Some of the women, peering down from their platforms of rock, stare at this son of Blish as he passes.

Some of them laugh. Their hunters would have killed the moose.

One or two men, sitting with their backs against the trees, mock at him, flinging the word for moose after him.

Carnack suddenly wishes to kill them.

He moves on, loiters by himself, looks up and down.

He hears them clucking and shouting behind him.

He lingers before Heetow's cave. Heetow is not there; does not come out.

He pushes out alone, up into the hills behind the cliff where the caves are, through a rift where a torrent has worn its way down, dragging his long spear up the weary gulch.

He keeps wanting to go back.

So we may see him setting out into the hills day after day. From The Rock. From The Hill.

Inkin, no doubt, is sometimes with him, to climb trees for birds' eggs, or to gather berries as they pass; to hunt for smaller animals with sticks and stones and clubs, and to help home with the kill—if Carnack makes one.

How he fares we cannot tell. The family circle does not perceptibly diminish in the glimpses that we get of it. Some of the anonymous ones, we may suppose, lend a hand.

As time passes we find him hunting with Heetow. They have forgotten Blish and his moose up at the caves; forgotten to laugh. Heetow, we may be sure, carries home his share of the spoil, for all that his father is a rich and mighty one.

A year or two later, or thereabouts, we find Carnack out with the veteran hunters, amongst whom it is not difficult to recognize Old Huckar by his huge, crooked thighs and bent knees, and Blozzip, by his hulking, hairy torso, helping them to kill a bear—the very beast, by the way, that some insist is no other than the cave bear himself, or an American equivalent.

Possibly Carnack hunts with them habitually now and we simply have no other pictures of it. Possibly a native skill and cunning have won him a place with them. Or perhaps, which seems more likely, the men have gone outside their accustomed ranks to recruit extra hands to take this particular bear, which appears to be a monstrous one. Or it may even be that Carnack himself first finds the brute; tracks him to his lair, and goes off to Shoulder Hill for help; sees his great tawny hulk behind a rock, or catches sight of him moving in amongst the trees of an opposite slope as he himself is stalking down some cañon; creeps up on him, poises for a cast of the spear, and then thinks better of it—fortunately.

The beast has already destroyed one of his assailants when we are admitted to the scene. Carnack is sufficiently graphic about that. The victim lies between the paws of the snarling animal with his head crushed in. You are not permitted to escape the fact; the head is as flat as a flint. Huckar is seen on top of a nearby boulder offering to return the compliment with a rock of enormous proportions poised at arm's length above his head, ready to be brought down upon the skull of the animal. Blozzip, bristling, brawny, is seeking advantage for a blow with a club as thick as a man's leg. Others weave about, shouting, with rocks and clubs and spears. Several javelins hang in the animal's sides.

And where is Carnack? Stealing up with a spear, already within reach of a sweep from the very paw that has done for the man between the monster's feet. Blozzip's threat with the club is engaging the beast's attention while Carnack tries to drive the spear under its elbow.

Carnack, I think, is rather outdoing himself in this affair. He seems for the moment the bravest of them all, the most aggressively daring. Of course,

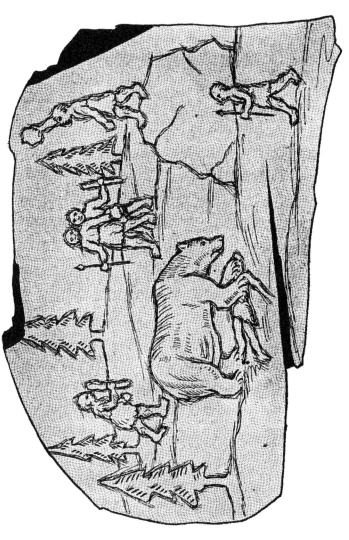

The Beast Had Already Destroyed One of His Assailants, When We Are Admitted to the Scene. Huckar Is on Top of a Boulder, with a Huge Rock Poised above His Head. Blozzip with a Club as Thick as a Man's Leg.

he drew the picture. Possibly he is out, in this hunt, not for glory and applause—I imagine they seldom gave that to each other—nor yet for immediate bear meat, but with a hope of gaining admittance to the hunting fraternity as an acceptable partner, a worthy member of groups going down to the basin, where one man alone, or even two or three together, could do little against the fleet and delectable horse or the sturdy bison, opulent of food.

Who kills the bear we do not know. We do know, however, from a quaint little inset in the corner of the pictolith, preserved intact to us by rare good luck, that the hunters give Carnack a share of the meat, which he carries off to Boulder Rock, dripping, over his bare and sweaty shoulder.

His mother sits in the shadow of the cave entrance, idle, as he comes up. Inkin, Laa'aa, Starga, observe his return from the edge of the rock. Do they know what hazards he has been through? Does he tell them? Does Starga swell and float while he relates the story of his prowess?

That night they feed on bear's meat; Moox, Laa'aa, Starga, Inkin, all of them.

But tomorrow!

And the day after that!

All the tomorrows!

What does the young man think of it all by this time? Of all this killing and eating and eating and killing again? This huddling stupidly together in a musty cavern amidst the foul bones of animals one has devoured, waiting to devour another one? Is it just a part of life to him, as it is to the others? Is it all of life to him?

Sometimes I can see him at this period, out on the hunt, pause amongst the pines that march up the ridges and look afar off through their lacy canopy of needles to the high-tossed hills beyond, filling his lungs with their spice and pungency; or behold him, homeward bound, lingering on the summit of Shoulder Hill while the sun goes down behind the piled-up ranges to the westward; wondering, perhaps, what it is that he seems to want more than the meat he is bringing home; what he wants that the others do not seem to want; what makes him want it.

I can see him march up to the cave in the dusk, mount the shelving path at the corner of the rock, go in amongst his people, throw down the kill of the day, and draw apart while they fall upon it, sitting by himself at the edge of the boulder while the last pale, shallow grey fades out of the sky-pool and the fishes of the night begin to swim there with their twinkling scales.

The others creep into their harsh and reeking nest. Quiet settles over them. Out there lies the lake, a dim sheen, barely discernible, beyond the trooping company of pines whose serried stalks, deep in shadow now, trace a verticle pattern in black parallels across its faint gleam.

Off on the ridges where he has been today, down in the basin where he hunted yesterday, over in the little, high-perched valley where he will go tomorrow, undrneath the darkness and the hush, everything is as it always was and always will be, heedless of the night and of the day, of him and of the others, of their going and their coming, their being there or elsewhere.

Up at Shoulder Hill all the people are asleep. No man stirs. Night locks them fast.

He looks around into the cave behind him. Looks out across the lake; down to where Seafar Basin stretches out in solitude beyond the gorge; far off to the pulsing flare of Grash-po-Nash. Up the valley toward the settlement. Into the cave at his back. Up to the stars again.

He goes into the cave.

Moox, his mother, sleeps obscenely, spraddled out, making noises in her flat nose.

Inkin stirs.

He hears Laa'aa breathing.

And Starga.

And Grash-po-Nash, regurgitating with a throaty mutter.

He finds a place in the nest.

Curls up.

Sleeps with the rest.

An owl hoots. . . .

Chapter IX

He Does Not Like It Too Well

THERE is nothing further for us in the record until we emerge from the fractured, dislocated fragments picked up in the talus from whose meager information we have, with the assistance of intelligence reflected back upon them from later pictures, pieced out our story to this point. Henceforth we stand on the more solid ground, comparatively rich in continuity, correlation and detail, of the sheath of smooth, upright rock, high on the Utah cañon wall, where the hand of Carnack traced out the chronicle twenty-five thousand years ago and where most of it, we can believe, was still intact when we discovered it.

I can see him now, standing there before that table of stone, the ball of his firm hand flattened against the rock and pressed white as he holds his graving tool, delicately fashioned out of flint as Blish had taught him how to fashion it, to its smooth surface, tapping, tapping, tapping, easily and without haste; click, click, click with his hammer-stone;

one knee against the rock for steadiness, the other braced behind him; arms with free sweep of movement; deer skin garment loosened and thrown back or laid aside entirely on warm, pleasant days; shadow and light of rhythmic muscular action playing over arms, shoulder and back under his swart skin; radiant shafts from the high swinging sun striking down through the crisp leaves of oak that hang above the bench; flutter and dapple of silver and gold about his brow as the breeze sways through the branches; chin upthrust; eyes fixed wide; lank hair tossed back; slowly, slowly, here a little, there a little, line upon line, putting himself upon that rock for that there was within him something that he must set down; something he must say.

Now and then he stops to breathe deep of the sparkling air that comes puffing up the cañon, with merry leap from pine to dancing pine-top and to peer down into the soft blue, rugged depths below, or gaze across to the opposite ridges, swimming in a lambent sea of down-poured summer sunlight. Serrations in them let his vision pass beyond and wander over the plains of Seafar Basin, shimmering in a haze of silent heat, to the plastic bulk of tawny mountains that rim its border miles upon miles away.

On the grass beside him, with one ear cocked at his friend and master, lies Loof, the wolf-dog that nuzzled its cold nose into my hand on that moment-ous afternoon three years ago when I stood on that very spot—save that the spot itself has meanwhile been washed and blown away in the streaming cur-rents of the years—and led me to the master and the man.

I can see him thus, for thus he has drawn himself, in his own plain way, upon this very rock, disclosing at one stroke the secret of the pictoliths and trans-muting them into a crystal chaplet, illuminating the uplifted brow of the first, so far as we know, of the life-bringers. For it is in this picture that he stands revealed, that we learn the theme and thesis of his life and character; that we glimpse the poetic impulse of the man which he himself could feel but could not understand.

Judging from internal and collateral evidence which it is needless to go into here, our artist com-menced to incise his pictures on the rock when he was a young man of twenty odd. We have learned from examples of his earlier engravings found about the ancient cave site and in other places that he had been preparing himself for this undertaking—un-consciously, no doubt—since he was a lad by scribbling on random rocks in idle moments. Although most of these early specimens of his craftsmanship are crude in the extreme and some of them grotesquely unintelligible, those encountered in The Haunt exhibit a steadily progressive promise of the skilful execution finally achieved in the finished pictures on the parent rock. The minute gradations up to his last excellence, the missing links between promise and fulfillment, were either on the outer rim of the original wall and therefore the first to go and the most deeply buried in the rocky slide below, or were on free pieces which did not happen to be found; which would not be surprising, for only a few, all told, of these thumb-nail sketches were discovered.

The pictures seem to have originated without a plan or ultimate intention. They were, I feel, the occasional preoccupation of a more or less lonely man with busy hands and something going on within him. He had already come to frequent The Haunt habitually, apparently, when he began to set them down. The idea of making a complete record of his life grew up within him, I believe, if it ever were a fixed idea, as one well-remembered incident after another assumed thrilling similitude upon the wall before him under the instinctively creative touch, however fumbling, of his earliest haphazard efforts.

Perigord, Cassell and the rest disagree with me in this, holding that Carnack commenced his pictoliths on a carefully selected rock with deliberate purpose and a fully outlined plan; the plan and purpose being, not to tell the story of himself, but of his dog. They point, to support their view, to the dominating position of the picture of the dog which came off in my fingers from the top center rim that day, to the emphasis Carnack lays upon the dog from the moment that he appears upon the scene, and to the fairly close approach to serial orderliness which runs throughout the rock.

The observation by these experts of material data is exhaustive and correct, their deductions honest and immediate, their logic beyond challenge and their conclusions not to be gainsaid upon the premises. But they, I know, are wrong. They miss the spirit of the man, the inner hint of him, the timid deep disclosure of his very self.

They ride, it seems to me, to their conclusions, upon an unyielding track of logic within a train of steely thought wheeled with inelastic facts and propelled by cold reason; whereas soft-shod, excursive amblings down quiet lanes and in sequestered nooks in sentimental and intuitive mood are needed in the journey to the heart of things. Carnack flees from their scientific gaze as he would have fled from them if they had come upon him on his bench of rock some brilliant summer afternoon, whittling at his stone.

It is true that the dog, as we are to see, did play a part of the first importance in the life of Carnack. It may be that he did "run off with the story" as the saying is, later on. But he was incidental to it for a long time after he appeared, and wholly unknown to it before he comes over its horizon. If the pictures tell us anything they tell us this.

Carnack was at his picture-making, we can see, for six or eight years, bringing them down to date from time to time, no doubt. Then we strike a snag. The concluding pictures tell us that he left the country. But the events up to the moment of his going and the circumstances of his departure are related with particularity. From the manner of his leaving we know that he could not have stopped to put it all down before he went. But no other artist could have done it for him. There was no other artist, and no one else who knew what to put down. So we know that he must have come back again.

This is one of the considerations that leads me to the conclusion that the fossil bones of the prehistoric man found by Cassell in The Haunt on the

Fourth Expedition to the Seafar Basin were those of Carnack himself; returning, perhaps, to complete the record of the first phase of his life, or in loneliness—who knows?—to spend his last days amidst the scenes of his youth near the people who had cast him out.

Where had he been meanwhile? How long had he been gone? What had he been doing? What had become of Starga and Loof, and Pono, the horse that had gone with him? Why had he not included all this in the record that he came back to. finish?

The answer to these questions lies, I think, in differences both Cassell and Fischer were able to point out between the workmanship—"technique", they called it—in the pictures which he must have made after his return and those we can be certain that he drew before his departure. The later ones, these two experts showed me, were more skilfully done; more precise and even; finer in every way. The man had kept his hand in while he was away. He had learned even better how to draw upon the rocks! Somewhere there is rich treasure in store for the one who finds it, if he made his intervening record on stone as perdurable as the sheaf we found perched on the Utah cañon's cheek.

It is not to be assumed that he who runs may read this rock that Carnack carved, or that the wayfaring man, though wise, may not err therein, as we see when such experts disagree as Cassell and Perigord and Fischer. It is not all so simple and straightforward as it might seem from the easy assurance with which the interpretation is set forth here. Toward the end of the story the order grows and the sequence becomes less obscure, but over much of it the grouping was confused in the extreme. Nor was there any certain way to distinguish between a series and a single picture. Carnack used no rules or borders. Sometimes the sequence was in the vertical, sometimes in the horizontal. The artist did not hesitate to go back and make use of empty spaces passed over in the first instance when the ample reaches of the rock promised inexhaustibility, or his plans were humbler. These reversions always proved disturbing until this habit of anachronism was detected. Even then it was not always easy to determine just where a picture did fit in after you had discovered where it did not.

Neither is it to be assumed that each picture taken by itself was always obvious and direct in its statement of the facts to be derived from it, or that

its message bearing on the complete history was delivered as clearly as it is here repeated. Anyone
who will attempt to describe in one picture, or even
two or three, an event in his own life of high interest
and importance will see what limitations Carnack
labored under twenty-five thousand years ago, up
there against his rock; and will be able to arrive
at the difficulties of an interpreter in rendering the
picture back into the event, with its antecedents and
its consequences and its implications.

Carnack, furthermore, was sketchy and impres-
sionistic in the extreme in his technique. Three
radiating lines, for instance, are called upon to
represent sufficiently a shaggy head of hair; two are
made to do for a bison's mane; while we must be able
to know from four short, brusque, wavy, gash-like
strokes on Blozzip's breast that he was an Hairy
One.

Thus it was that the interpretation of the pictoliths of the Seafar Basin in western Utah was a
long, laborious and not always certain task, with
much going back and forth, much patching and
weaving together, many false starts, many full
stops, and many, many more than one glorious and
hardbuilt edifice dragged down in wreckage by an

unaccommodating picture half a span away or an inexorable line on a man's leg.

We can gather from the first pictures that we come to on the rim, ragged as they are, that Carnack has been faring better since the bear fight, a year or two before, in which we have seen him distinguishing himself. We have two pictures of him which show him hunting with the other cave men on even terms, apparently; although possibly all the men available have been called together in both cases for a communal drive. In one instance the cave men are invading The Basin and killing four bison which they have probably succeeded in cutting out of a larger herd. In the other a similar party is butchering a band of elk which they have surrounded at a water hole; in the fall, apparently, for the trees are leafless, though the snow has not yet come. No doubt this was a memorable occasion, insuring a good supply of meat to begin the winter on, for the elk are numerous, and the weather would permit their leaving the meat around until they could eat it up. Skihack, with his retreating forehead and advancing jaws, appears in both these scenes, with Blozzip and Old Huckar, still the grizzled master of them all. Palupe, too, is with them, and Heetow, his son; the Noseless One.

Carnack hunts with Heetow, also. A picture on the rim reveals the two slaughtering a colt; a pitiful little animal; hacking it to pieces with flint knives. They have ventured forth into The Basin, where alone the horse is found, leaving the valley, no doubt, in the dead of night, to be on the ground in time to catch the animals at their early grazing, if fortune is with them.

Carnack likewise hunts alone. He tells us of a boar which he kills singlehanded; evidently a narrow squeak for him, with the chances on the boar's side more than once, to judge from pieces of broken spears and clubs lying about and what seems to be meant for blood streaming from what could be a gash in Carnack's leg. He finally despatches the beast, whom he represents as unduly monstrous, with a random rock picked up from the battle-ground after his weapons are done for.

Side by side with this drawing is another one describing, apparently, the return from this very boar hunt. It is interesting in the glimpse it gives us into the cave at this time. Carnack is discovered climbing up the notched path to the top of the boulder with the animal over his shoulder; a feat from which we may appraise this people's strength of leg and back. The others are looking on; Inkin, a stout lad, full of curiosity and admiration; Starga, plump and blooming, and the leaner Laa'aa, almost ready to mate, watching; Moox squatting off at one side, staring; with some of the anonymous in the background, who seem to be taking it more as a matter of course than we might expect, that Carnack should be bringing home a boar singlehanded. The animal is drawn smaller than it was while he was killing it. No doubt it seemed smaller to him dead than alive, and he draws it so, illogically accepting the impression for the fact.

The next winter is a hard one. It is the one which Carnack is reporting in the cave scene which we have described as typical of family life in the winter time. The season sets in early, we may assume, with a succession of storms. The drift which we have seen forms across the entrance of the cave. Snow gathers deep in the cañons. Deer and elk come down from the ridges and trek to the basins. Small game is scarce and difficult to take. Starvation soon stalks down the whistling wind and hovers in the swirling snow. Starvation, and a misery of cold.

Matters grow so serious that Carnack has to undertake a journey to the basin in the dead of winter.

Inkin goes with him.

Carnack Climbing up the Notched Path to the Top of
the Boulder, with a Slain Boar over His Shoulder.

Evidently it was an event of the first magnitude
in Carnack's eyes partly, perhaps, because of the
hazard in it, and partly because he felt the issues of
life and death in its outcome.   He draws it large
upon the rock.   First we have a picture of the prep-
aration; Carnack overhauling javelins and spears
for himself and Inkin in the half light of the bitter
winter's day under the scant shelter of the overhanging cave.   Flakes of snow are floating down
through the grey air.   It is difficult to handle flints
and thongs with numb fingers.   Carnack may have
learned to blow on them to keep them warm.   No
doubt he knows how to thrust his hands into his arm
pits from time to time or hold them under his fur
garments for a while.   Perhaps he stops to wrap his
skins more closely about him now and then; tries to
cover his bare arms and blue, aching feet a little
with the loose, stiff, hairy skirts.   They have no
place to retreat to, these people, no warmth anywhere to go to and revive themselves.   No surcease.
No respite.   They must wait for the slow processes
of spring.

The second picture shows him and Inkin on their
way down through the valley toward the gorge and
the basin in the storm.   They have crawled out of
their nests in the drifting dark to be in the basin by

daylight. It will soon be night again. Snow is fluttering down, as it has been for days. They hear the faint rustle of it as they climb down the rock in front of the cave; feel it in the air; on their faces and knees and shoulders. They would do better to wait for fair weather, but who knows when that will be? They can wait no longer. Barefooted and bareheaded they slide down the path from the top of the boulder, packed hard and icy, assisting themselves with the butts of their spears, and strike out through the darkness.

Snow lies deep on the levels and gathers in snowdrifts. But the men from the caves have tracked a way through it; Blozzip and Skihack, Palupe, Old Huckar, going down to the basin in bands. The footing is uneven and lumpy under their bare soles. They leave the lake to one side, a broad, flat field of sheer white, unscarred by a footstep.

The trail through the gorge, terrific even in summer time, is icy and hidden; precipitous, treacherous. The snow slants into the cañon in hard-driven lines, stinging and blinding, striking dizzily down to the river bed. They struggle and stumble along, Carnack ahead.

Here the third picture catches them.

Soon they look out on the basin, afloat with un-

ceasing snowflakes. It would be good to turn back.
But to what? Day after day like the present one,
with starvation coming closer and closer? They
push out upon the broad expanse, empty and track-
less, knee-deep in snow, playground of the blizzard
and snowstorm.

The fourth picture shows their reward. They
have overtaken a bison, perhaps a sick or starving
straggler, floundering through the snowdrifts, and
are prodding it to death with their spears, beating it
with clubs. Their javelins hang in the animal's
sides, where Carnack has flung them in the first
assault. How long it takes them to subdue the
beast to its last bubbling, quivering sigh upon the
trodden snow is not important after all these years.

They satisfy themselves forthwith, we may be
sure, hacking into the hot flesh of the beast, shouting
and screaming. Then comes the weary way homeward, jubilant and exhausted, stage by stage, bringing up the meat in relays, saving it all; over the
plain, up the gorge, across the valley, up the face of
the rock, through the storm and the drifts. Picture
five of the series outlines all this for us.

It was a great event; a desperate crisis met and
overcome; a turning point, perhaps, in Carnack's
manhood. He writes it large.

They all come through the winter, apparently, alive, unless one or two of the nameless ones are missing. We learn this from a picture, half on the tablet and half lost, celebrating some event of the following spring, which gives us a glimpse into the cave. But they all show signs of wear. Moox, especially, is lean and dry, even for her.

The purport of the picture cannot be determined. The climax, so to speak, is on the missing portion, which is rather annoying, for those we see are gazing over at the focal point with every indication that something was going on there that we would like to know about. Carnack evidently is the center of it, being absent from the portion that is left.

Perhaps—but speculation is quite pointless.

Chapter X

He Finds Refuge in the Haunt

SPRING comes at last, pouring down from a
bluer sky, welling up from a softer, warmer
earth; brimming and balmy; releasing the tension
in muscle and skin; dissolving the snow; filling the
rivers and fields and the forests; filling the veins of
young Carnack.

Blozzip and the others now pad past again on
springy turf on their way to the lake and the basin.
The ice is all gone and the leaves are all out and
game is abundant; ducks passing northward; elk
and deer returning to their higher haunts; horse
and bison in the basin moving toward the fresh,
green hillsides.

Carnack goes and kills, and returns again, unsatisfied. He walks down by the brook, stands
under the pines, stands under the stars in the night;
stands, in the dawn, on the rock, looking off.

He can hear, as he stands in the shadow of the cliff
behind him, a brook running down amidst the stones
and sedges of a little valley that he knows about;

see the wisps of mist caught in its grasses; recall its trees stretching up their arms and spreading out their fingers for the sun to come; sense the hush and tender fragrance of it as he gazes over to where it lies, high on a far-off ridge; secluded, quiet, calm, content.

Then, on a day, he sets out, just as the others begin to creep out of the nest one by one to turn over the bones of the evening before for gristles and meatshreds.

Starga stares at him, standing there, over a bit she has found. He looks this way and that; looks at her; moves to the edge of the rock; climbs down its ladder-like path; reaches the ground and strikes off.

Starga, chewing, stopping to swallow, watches him move toward the cluster of pines on swift, soft strides; lightly bent; slightly slouched; head on a level; eyes straight ahead. Moox casts a glance after him. He does not look back.

He enters the cluster of pines, turns into the path that leads round the head of the lake, not yet beaten as flat and as hard as it will be.

He hears, in the distance, the rising cackle of the men at Shoulder Hill; the squealing of the women.

He lifts his face to the golden peaks where the

sun is striking now; the distant western ridges where The Haunt lies hidden.

A silvery mist films the lake and valley floor, its tattered edges floating into the purple shadows that still cling to the feet of the encircling hills.

He comes to the river and wades it. It is shallow and sluggish where it broadens to enter the lake. The gold on the ridges is turning to delicate amber. The mists are dispersing. Sunrise is creeping into the western rim of the valley, joyous and brilliant, radiant, glowing.

He hears hunters going down the trail he has just left behind, through the pines, to the Gorge; Old Huckar's growl, Skihack's staccato cackle and click.

He reaches the creek that comes in where the flint is. He scoops up a handful of water and drinks. What spills runs unheeded down his chin and his neck and the tender hair on his breast.

He looks around; out across the pale blue lake, beginning to ruffle in the bouncing morning breeze that has come down from the ridges. Down to the Gorge. Back at the crest of Shoulder Hill, towering high above the oaks about its feet. The caves are invisible and out of earshot. The sunlight is almost upon him.

He sets his face to the west and strikes off in a long, swinging gait, hips free, shoulders slouched, knees slightly bent; half a walk; half a trot. But first he picks up some flints; three nodules, carefully chosen; three small ones.

He leaves the head of the lake and turns off toward a ridge that reaches out, like a huge lion's paw, with spread claws, into the broadened valley where the lake has gathered.

The path has disappeared in the gravel.

The shards crunch and grit and give way under his bare soles. Clusters of harsh bottom grass whip about his naked shins, cutting at them. He is watchful for snakes. His three flint nodules are in his hand; compassed by a grasp of outstretched fingers—strong, muscular, brown, whitened at spots of pressure on the stones. Three in one hand, tirelessly, all the way up the mountains to The Haunt, now four or five miles away.

He circles the claws of the ridge, keeping to the slanting valley floor, tipped up against the hills.

He strikes for the head of a little meadow shut in by two ridges. As it narrows down, the semblance of a path appears. In another moment the walls have closed in and the trail begins its climb up the cañon to get across the ridge.

The sun is on him, hot and clear. The air is heavy with perfume of blossom and bush, plants underfoot and distant pines; aromatic, pungent, intoxicating. He inhales deep, tingling breaths of it. Bees buzz and drone past, heavy with honey or hunting it.

There is a little stream. It leaps over ledges and laughs; hides behind rocks and chuckles.

Spurning the sand and small rock of the hillside with bent, clutching toes, digging in for purchase at each upward step, he begins the ascent; abrupt, twisting, now along the cañon wall, now on the flanking ridge, now in the creek bed, but always up and up. The sun shining down on him. Sweat under his eyes, on his neck.

He follows the ridge to its root, not stopping to look as he goes but nevertheless drinking in the scene and the hot, spicy air; follows up the parent ridge, dips down from it suddenly into the next cañon, the trail all the way defined for his accustomed feet, though blind, no doubt, to such as we; threads across it, clambers up the other side, and pursues his way.

A mountain lion breaks covert and sweeps gracefully off, disappearing in a few swift bounds.

Carnack, head straight forward—we have the

very picture—shoulders slightly slouched, knees slightly bent, toes crunching into the loose roughness of the going, puts rod after rod behind him.

He strikes up the second ridge, crosses the head of the succeeding cañon, too rough and steep to be crossed lower down, follows out its opposite ridge, goes down a branch of it, pitches into the next cañon —Picture Cañon; a large one—follows it down for a space, swings off across it, and mounts the farther wall. Here climbing begins again; stiff, steep work over the rocks, with now and then a hand thrust out to catch at a bush or a root or an outcrop.

He begins to hear the waterfall shouting at him.

He reaches the cascades below it.

He comes amongst ferns and moist growing things.

He catches a glimpse of the tumbling water, rushing and dazzling; hissing through the air excitedly; struggling, holding back; letting go, leaping to the dash below.

Up into the drifting spray of it; through a tumble of wet rocks, mossy and black.

And so, suddenly, into the opening of the little valley above the waterfall.

The Haunt!

A lone wolf slinks up the gulch at the head of it,

stopping every step or two to look over its shaggy shoulder at him.

A deer bounds away from the spring.

An eagle swings through the sky, alone, and screams that he is there.

The trees laugh and whisper to each other that he has come again.

Little birds flutter and chirrup and settle again, talking it over.

The brook, rustling by to the waterfall and the cañon and the Basin and the clouds again, calls out to him a welcome and a parting.

He stands, and looks around.

It must have been a charming place. It still has a magical attractiveness, seared and withered as it is. What is was in Carnack's day, with its quiet scattered trees and parklike clusterings of shrubbery with open sward between—Carnack tries to represent it in his drawings—its embracing walls of brilliant saffron and green rock shutting off approach except by the narrow trail up the steep slopes of Picture Cañon below and through the gulch at its head, its gentle slope and cool, restful brook, its sheltered nooks and little vistas, we do not find it difficult to imagine.

The ridges above—both Cassell and Fischer

agree with Perigord in this—were pleasantly tim-
bered with fine conifers; several kinds of pines; firs;
some cedars. Carnack shows us these in his pictures.
It was a petrified survivor of this forestation that
the boys and I found in the gulch above The Haunt
when we were exploring a way out of the little valley
on our first sojourn there. Why one alone of a
considerable company should have been singled out
for preservation in resplendent, parti-colored onyx
I shall have to leave to M. Perigord and his geologists for explanation.

Oaks grew in cozy groups about The Haunt itself. Bushes trooped down from the encircling hills
and the crests of flanking ridges onto the floor of
the valley in adventurous thickets, a-twitter with
birds. The brook, fed by ample springs fully
stored with melting winter snows, brimmed its way
in solid swirls down the sunny center of the vale,
midrib to a feather of green waving grasses that
delicately brushed the feet of the valley's walls. At
the lowest lips of the valley's mouth the brook
plunged a sheer hundred feet into Picture Cañon
in what must have been a delightful waterfall, and
cascaded down two or three hundred more, filling
The Haunt and the bench where Carnack later
worked odd times at his pictoliths with the soothing,

ceaseless plash of busy water rushing amongst rocks. The spring still found alive today in the charming nook where the tributary gulch comes in was then a bubbling pool. We can recognize its location in the pictoliths. Here it was, by its cool sides, lush with soft grasses and immaculate with gravel, that Carnack chipped his flints; here, underneath a clump of trees that stood against the rocky wall behind, he built his hut. Here Loof came to him. Here the long course of their attachment for each other worked itself out, the first exercise of that true dominion over every living thing that moveth upon the earth which was God's gift to man, and to the animal, before Adam was formed of the dust of the ground and had called this animal a ravenous wolf to be dreaded and destroyed.

Here he has one of his fierce set-tos with the hairy Blozzip. Here he learns the use of fire, and first uses it. Here Starga joins him at a juncture in her life and his. Here, as I believe, he returns to die, full of memories, full of years, perhaps. And here Perigord, Fischer, Cassell and myself, led to the spot by his own pictures of it made twenty-five thousand years before on the wall just outside the valley's mouth, found living traces of him; flint spear, javelin, and arrowheads; a glorified

form of coup-de-poing which might easily have been
used with a handle as an axe; a hammer-stone or
two of iron pyrites; half worked fragments of flint;
an abundance of chips; implements of one kind and
another, amongst them several of his graving tools
and what Fischer took to be a needle of flint used
for sewing skins together, as we find Carnack doing
later; some of the sketches we have spoken of;
bones and deer horns, a few of them carved slightly
—he seems to have preferred the harder stone—and
an attempt at a figurine in stone which had turned
out to be, unintentionally, of course, a grotesque.
His sense of form and proportion, sufficiently
marked in his pictoliths to evoke enthusiastic com-
ment from both Perigord and Fischer, failed him
in the third dimension. He must have been aware
of this, for we find only this one attempt in the
round.

We had merry arguments, the three of us, before
our tent doors in The Valley of the caves, as to what
the sculpture was supposed to celebrate. Perigord
was sly and somewhat Parisian over it. Fischer,
who found it, unbent jovially before it—to incite
me, I used to think, to the partisan defense of Carnack I was always ready for. Excepting two com-
plex rectangular games of solitaire which he played

with a fixed face and grim self-control immediately after dinner every evening, and occasional misadventures which befell his adversaries in learned argument, the figurine was his sole relaxation during our summer with Carnack and his people. The figurine, still unexplained, is now a part of the Fischer collection of the Utah Pictoliths in the Hamburg Museum, where it may be seen, along with specimens of Carnack's flint handicraft and other items, by anyone who goes that way. The reproduction in this book is from a faithful facsimile supplied by the Museum.

The sense of seclusion and shelter still felt in this hill-encircled niche must always have been present, but The Haunt could scarcely have been either a secret place or an entirely private retreat in the days when Carnack first resorted to it. It lay on the direct route from The Valley of the Caves to much rich hunting country on Southwest Divide, and to Volcano Basin, where Grash-po-Nash was then active and where the cave people, as we have seen, had errands other than their hunting.

Other routes to Volcano Basin may have been in use at the time. Novices that we were, the boys and I located several possible passes over the main divide from Cavern Cañon and The Valley; but

a glance at the map will show that the one through
The Haunt might easily have been the favorite one.
The climb from the cañon below was not a difficult
one as climbs went for these aboriginals. The trail
was an obvious and easy one up the gulch at the
head of the little valley and across the ridge into the
next cañon—Three Quarters Cañon, as it is now
called, for reasons known only to its unknown
godfather, apparently—whose headwaters lie
against the divide between Seafar and Volcano
basins, and which is now taken advantage of by the
motor highway as a pass from one to the other; the
very pass the boys and I had rolled through that
momentous afternoon, all unconscious of those
others whom we were shortly to discover who had
been that way so long before us.

This route was well watered, it cut off much distance as well as altitude, and there was always an
excellent chance, no doubt, of finding game in The
Haunt itself as they passed by, either at the spring,
which must have been used as a water-hole from
the ridges for miles around in seasons of low water,
or in the lush pasturage along the brook. Indeed,
this alone must often have brought hunters to The
Haunt as a destination in itself.

This popular feature of The Haunt must have

brought Carnack into frequent collision with the people of the caves when he first began to make it his personal retreat. Whether, in time, he asserted an undisputed lordship over it is a question that is in dispute. I rather think he did. That, at least, is my interpretation of a picture of a brush Carnack shows himself to have had with none other than his brother Skihack, in which the two are going at it hammer and tongs. I imagine it was a serious and exciting affair; at the entrance to the valley; near the waterfall, where either might easily be pushed over. Carnack literally is using his hammer-stone on his brother; which, I am afraid, he was not sorry for a chance to do. The outcome speaks better for Skihack's skull than it does for Carnack's fraternal sentiments, for we find the older brother later on still in possession of his life and Carnack of The Haunt.

Chapter XI

He Sets Up in Business

CARNACK began to resort to The Haunt habitually two or three years after the record emerges from the chaos of the broken pieces in the talus into the comparative order and clarity of the fixed tables on the rock.

He was a young man of twenty odd by this time; just turning into manhood. This, at least, is the age Perigord and I arrived at. Cassell, I believe, makes him younger. It does not seem to me especially important.

Pictures of the period show him to have been a lively and muscular young fellow, quite capable of taking care of himself, one may judge. His legs have the notable development by which he is identified in his pictoliths, a factor not unimportant in a tussle. His shoulders and arms are good, with a long reach. This advantage, perhaps, would not have proved so pronounced in those days as in our own, as I imagine they knew nothing of the modern punch.

He was somewhat oversized; not so large as Blozzip, who far outhulked them all by this time, but larger than most of the others. He must have been strong for his size, for later we find him surviving a really ferocious encounter with Blozzip himself, coming out of it with all his members unimpaired and with that terrible fellow's perennial respect, apparently, if not affection.

His legs are straight and braced against the ground, without that crook of the knee, exaggerated to a caricature in Old Huckar, which we find in most of the race. His shoulders slouch a little; his head is thrust forward; but again to a lesser degree than his fellows. The jaws are firm, but not prognathous, as are Skihack's; the chin well set, somewhat receding; the cheek bones high; the eyes rather larger and fuller than most, although not so deep. The head is taller and longer than we might expect, with a forehead not too slanting.

Thus, at least, Cassell reconstructs him from the cranial bones found in The Haunt, and thus his pictures show him.

All this disturbs the experts. From Carnack's pictures of himself—drawn better than those he makes of the other, excepting Starga; from reflections he has studied in the fishing pool, no doubt, from his shadow as he passes, from a sense of form and features gained in a thousand ways—they cannot classify and catalogue him neatly in any savage category. He should have been featured and constructed otherwise. He sticks out, so to speak, around the edges of the pattern. The high cheek bones suggest the Esquimaux, but nothing else about him does. Certain points are prophetic of the Aztec, but he was far from being one. He had the cliff-dweller's jaws, but a better forehead. There is promise, for the moment, of the Sioux Indian, but it is repudiated by a second glance. No steady trace, in fact, of any race found in America, or elsewhere, is revealed in Carnack's form or features; nothing but an early sign, which the experts will not see, of the will of God, forcing its resistless way even then through human consciousness.

This is what is so disturbing to the scientists. The human mind must paste its set of labels on the things that pass before it. It must sort each one into a bin with a ready, made-up name on the lid. It must, by analysis and criticism, relate every new idea that presents itself in its own identity fresh from God to some group that has been deprived of any identity; whereas the only true relationship of an idea, if it is one, is to the Mind which conceived both it and all the others.

Cassell, I understand, is writing a book for the purpose of fastening a name on this "living creature", as Adam did upon the animals in the Garden of Eden as they passed before him; but what he calls Carnack or where he places him can be of no possible interest or importance. Carnack was Carnack, and his people were themselves. What more is possible or needful? You are you and I am I and I AM hath sent us both to take our place in His scheme of things. What else is there to any one of us that is true or consequential?

The first picture identifying Carnack with The Haunt is one which shows him making flints there; squatting underneath a tree in his favorite spot, where the spring came down out of the little side gulch; tapping away at them, with an untouched nodule at his side. He puts both the spring and the tree in his picture, just as they are today. Another tree, of course. Not even a lineal descendant of Carnack's tree after all these centuries. Although its heir. But the spring is the same, changed only in its volume, which is a mere dribble now at most seasons of the year, and the margin of green growth about it.

We do not need these features, however, to tell us that it is The Haunt. Carnack has given us a sign by which to know it; a symbol which he uses in every picture located there. In size it is no bigger, as a rule, than a thumb nail. In shape it is like a V with the lower half lopped off, or the bowl of a tall dipper. Something resembling a tree, highly conventionalized, rises from the bottom of it; and three, sometimes four, occasionally two, or even one, wavering lines depend from it.

This sign, recurring here and there throughout the pictoliths without apparent meaning or purpose, proved a great puzzle to us until we noticed that every time we definitely fixed a picture in The Haunt we found this symbol in a corner of it. Working from this broad hint and taking the queer lines in good faith as a tree, the truncated V became a cañon with a tree growing in it, the wavering lines a waterfall, and the whole thing a mark employed by Carnack to identify The Haunt itself. For where else was there a cañon with trees growing in it and concluding in a waterfall?

The varying number of lines in the waterfall made things difficult at first. But when we determined that it was a waterfall, and the conclusion satisfied the terms of the equation, their changing number took on a significance of the first importance and became later on a key to the very climax of Carnack's history. For their number clearly indicated stages of the water in the stream and served both as a calendar and a report on the weather.

Carnack has need by this time of all the flints that he can make.

Something has happened—to him, and to the world.

The story is given us in two pictures, and a sequel.

In the first picture Old Huckar has laid Carnack low and is walking off with the young man's spear.

In the second Carnack has laid Old Huckar low and is walking off with the carcass of a deer that the old fellow was fetching home for his four fat wives.

In the light of subsequent developments it is not difficult to determine what has happened.

Carnack, let us say, on a day goes a hunting. He has made a new spearhead and fastened it on.

Whither he fares we are not informed, and it is not important.

On the way he meets Old Huckar.

Huckar is hurrying home in the midst of the day from the hunt.

He has broken his spearhead and come back for another.

He is not in too good a temper. He has had to abandon the hot trail of a buck, or leave off from a big band of elk, or give up the hope of an antelope.

He spies young Carnack, with his spear. He espies his new spearhead, trim, slender and keen, with a muscular strength built up in its shoulder and throat. Everyone knows that Carnack is expert at spearheads.

He trots up to Carnack, confronts him and stops him; squat legs well apart. He looks at the spear and thrusts out his paw with a gesture and grunt of demand.

Carnack holds the spear out of reach and growls back at him.

Huckar bellows and roars; rushes in, and lays hold of it.

Carnack hangs on; Huckar falls on him.

They grapple and struggle; sturdy blows; tusslings and tearings with tooth and with talon.

Carnack is laid low, and the old fellow squaddles off into the hills again with the spear.

No doubt it has happened before. No doubt the cave hunters plundered Blish all his life.

But this time it turns out to be different.

Old Huckar comes back from the hills laden with a deer he has slaughtered.

Carnack waylays him; taps Old Huckar on the head with a club from behind a bush as he passes; and takes the deer away from him.

But he lets him keep the spear.

Therein is the point.

He does not take the spear back again, but the meat Old Huckar killed with it!

He lets Old Huckar keep the spear with which to get more meat for him!

If there were any doubt about the meaning of these pictures it would be cleared up by the sequel. This is quite an elaborate tableau. Carnack is seen seated in state on top of Boulder Rock, with Moox, Laa'aa, Starga, Inkin and the rest in a semi-circle around him. They are all eating heartily. Unconsumed meat is piled up before them; denuded bones form a heap at one side.

Up one corner of the rock we see Blozzip, Skihack, Palupe, mount, bearing flesh on their shoulders, fresh from the kill. Down the other descend Old Huckar, and two or three others I do not identify, without any meat on their shoulders, but carrying flints in their hands; finished flints. Carnack writes them large, so that there shall be no mistake about it.

It is not to be supposed, of course, that the scene on the rock is a literal one, or that the men from Shoulder Hill habitually filed up one side of Boulder Rock carrying supplies and down the other bearing away flints. Carnack is indulging in descriptive allegory, as he often does.

Nor need it be assumed that the transactions were always as docile and mutually pleasant as the one depicted here. No doubt Carnack had at first to let the idea of barter into most of their heads, as he had into Huckar's, with a club; although the prestige of having tackled Huckar may have stood him in good stead with the rest. But that is not the point. The point is that the idea has caught on. It has gotten through. It has taken hold. Carnack's flints are most desirable. One can get one if one fights Carnack for it— perhaps. But if one wishes one, all one has to do is to give Carnack sufficient meat for it, or a skin or two. So why fight? He will get the meat or the skin anyway. Why go to the trouble—and the risk? Why not give him a piece of deer meat, or a bear skin, in the first place, and get one?

They do; and the first step is taken toward the

CARNACK TAPS OLD HUCKAR ON THE HEAD WITH A CLUB; AND TAKES THE DEER
AWAY FROM HIM.

civilized state; the first step in mutual usefulness and benefit, in coöperation and exchange of service, in the brotherhood of man which is the thread and hue and fabric of our life together here.

Society has crossed the threshold of human experience and stands, the promised bride of man, with gentle, forbearing hand outstretched to beckon and assist him.

And Carnack has need of all the flints that he can make.

Why he goes to The Haunt to make them is another question.

Fischer maintains that he was compelled to; that his dickering in spearheads and living off the efforts of the others had turned them against him and they had driven him forth from the community. Cassell, with reservations, and allowances for Fischer, and divinations of his own, supports him. Perigord is not so sure.

I think that he is wrong. No doubt Carnack has made himself unpopular. No doubt the others resented his sitting around at home with his flints while they bore the burden and heat of the day. It is even possible that his skill in making flints, and the number he could turn out, or his facing of Old Huckar, or his compelling them to give him flesh for flints, frightened them in some confused and occult way; although I think that form of fear of him was aroused much later.

But there is another reason why he carried his heavy nodules of flint all the weary way from the place where they were found at the head of the lake, up across Catamount Ridge, down through Middle Creek Cañon, out over Razor Back, deep into Picture Cañon, and so to the little flat behind the waterfall.

It was the charm and beauty of the place, its quietude, serenity, and peacefulness, that drew him all that toilsome way. A disappointed longing for something which he had been looking for in his people, a groping hunger for an answer which they could not give him but which the silence and the solitude of this secluded mountain spot seemed to whisper in his eager ears. A solitary search for he knew not what, a lonely struggle, away out there at the front of time,toward a dim, far-burning light which he had glimpsed that day when he first found them all in their caves at Shoulder Hill, but which he was now beginning to see was not shining through them or their life beneath the cliffs, and which had not yet tipped with promise any of the dull and down-thrust faces in the circling cave at Boulder Rock.

For this man was a poet, with the lonely hungry heart of one, the up-turned, out-gazing eyes of one, seeking for the God that made him so.

Meanwhile affairs at home have taken a turn for the better. Carnack's flints are bringing in more meat than he could kill, and the family is prospering. Moox assumes a faint rotundity never even hinted at before, Starga grows more buxom, and Laa'aa's sagging cheeks fill out. Inkin begins to shoot up. And the others are hale and hearty. It is true that the number of anonymous ones seems to have diminished, but those that are missing, I have always assumed, have either been dropped from the records as superfluous to the narrative as it proceeds and too much bother, or have found their ways in life and departed upon them.

Carnack, as the chief provider, seems to be the master at home. We see him in one picture laying about him amongst the nameless ones with a bison bone. Just why is not apparent. I have always suspected that Starga is, innocently enough, at the bottom of it. She, at least, is in the picture, sitting alone, off at one side, looking on with evident approval.

It is not impossible that some of the others have been intruding too urgently upon her privacy. This opens up a large subject. Is Carnack recognizing and supporting the abstract principle of the right of each one to himself but not to the others, or is he saving her for himself?

The same question comes up later when we find Blozzip, the Hairy One, loitering about the cave at Boulder Rock and see Carnack driving him away with his bow and arrow. Of course Blozzip might have been on another errand than to run off with Starga. Fischer cites this picture amongst others in support of his contention that Carnack was a hunted outcast of the tribe. We cannot tell.

Still later we find Carnack raiding Blozzip in his own cave up at Boulder Hill; a feat of towering audacity unless, as has been hinted, and I am convinced, these people came, through failure to understand him, to feel a mystic awe of Carnack. Nothing less than such an awe of him can account for many things that happen, and that do not happen, up to the time when the very desperation of this fear, against which all the weapons of their warfare were without avail, drove them together in the final act of terrified expulsion.

Starga's responsible connection with this raid is

more than hinted at, I feel, in a picture which we have so close to the scene we are speaking of that the two might be companion pieces, in which Starga and Carnack are seen squatting in front of each other on the top of the rock. If these two are doing anything they are conversing. Starga clearly is making signs.

In the very next picture that we have amongst the pictoliths, in a certain direction from this one—as I have said, direction is not always conclusive of sequence, nor juxtaposition of relationship—Carnack is seen at the entrance to Blozzip's cave. Blozzip is standing up to him. Their attitudes are threatening; but there is no fight, at this time, or the artist would have told us so. Has Blozzip been prowling about the cave at Boulder Rock again, casting appraising glances at the blooming Starga? Has Starga complained of him to Carnack? If so, why? Why to Carnack? As the older brother, the natural protector? Or as something else, wished for?

One of Blozzip's wives is sitting in the shadow of the cave, looking on, with a baby in her lap and arms. The infant is plainly perishing; whether from cold or starvation due to the mother or from an injury we cannot tell. The mother is gazing at Carnack; beseechingly, we can imagine, from a certain angle in her posture and a line on her cheek; a screwed-up look beneath her out-stretched eyes which might be due as much to accident as to design on the part of the artist.

Is she pleading for her husband, or is there a hint here which leaves the other picture, of Starga and Carnack, hanging in the air unexplained? Has Carnack come—perhaps at Starga's instigation!— to heal the child? Does he know that it need not die? That is beyond belief. Or has he some frightful potion for it; some filthy, hideous mixture to rub on; some prehistoric vaccine? Whatever Carnack's errand, Blozzip makes his stand against it. He does not seem to be concerned about the child. Possibly, with four wives on hand, and a fifth in mind, a child or two less would not seem a calamity.

If Carnack is saving Starga for himself, if a mutual romance is burgeoning between these two, we have no other hints of it. Carnack gives us one drawing of Starga at this time dressing skins on top of the rock which Perigord, viewing the entire discussion in well bred amusement, lightly maintains is a love sonnet extolling the virtues and charms of the maiden; an explanation which others choose to take more seriously than he does. All

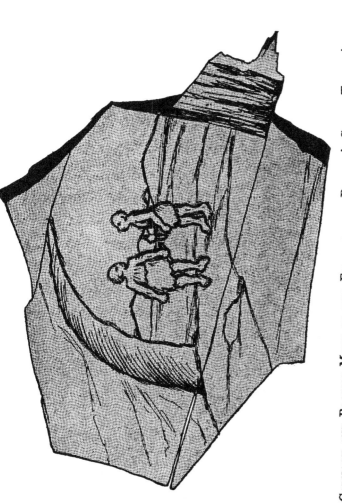

CARNACK AND BLOZZIP MEET AT THE ENTRANCE OF BLOZZIP'S CAVE. THEIR ATTI-
TUDES ARE THREATENING; BUT THERE IS NO FIGHT, OR THE ARTIST
WOULD HAVE TOLD US SO.

that Carnack was intending was to inform us that the family now had plenty of skins as well as food, or that Starga was especially expert at dressing them, or that he has worked out and taught her a new method of treating them to make them soft, which she is executing. This, I think, is the true rendering of the scene; for we soon find him arrayed in garments that fall and cling and drape more than the former harsh, stiff hides he wore—and which the others are still seen in.

At another time he shows her nursing Moox, to all appearances, through an illness. Moox is lying on the ground. We do not know why. She may have eaten too much—may be paying the penalty, in a prehistoric way, of prosperity. Starga squats beside her with an object in her hands doing something to the patient with it. It is a great pity we do not know what the object is or what she is doing with it, or what ailed Moox, for the patient recovers. We see her for many years more. Where Laa'aa is during this illness Carnack does not inform us. She is not permanently absent, however, as we are to learn.

Some maintain, in spite of complete lack of any evidence, that Starga was already Carnack's; that they could not have lived together in a cave without falling into such relationship. The inference is incorrect. The facts, as we are permitted to read them, do not support such an assumption. The question of the morality, or immorality, of these primitives has been pretty thoroughly mouthed by certain students of the pictoliths with a bent of mind that makes them like to taste how others sin, without reward of savory morsels. The cave people of the Seafar Basin were not bothered much about the question. Nor did it bother them. They were not sufficiently advanced. There may have been, and doubtless were, what we would regard as lapses, but the lapses themselves or the suppressed or unsuppressed desires which they indicated did not seem to interest the others much. Carnack, at least, is quite silent on the subject.

We know that there was a plurality of wives, but apparently there was a form of constancy within the cave which ought to reassure the moralist on the ground that it may be a higher form of conduct to be faithful to four wives than false to one. We find one instance of a shift of wives—and, of course, Starga's eventual experience—but no others. Whether this conjugal fidelity was enforced by the club or by public opinion or sprang from the hearts of those concerned is something that we must guess, and that one may guess as freely as another. I am inclined to think that simple-heartedness, innocence, ignorance of good and evil, the absence of sophisticated suggestion to do otherwise, was at the bottom of it. They were like children, these primitives, it is to be remembered, wholly; not yet knowing enough about themselves to trouble themselves about themselves.

In any case, Carnack is not a very anxious or attentive lover, for we find him spending more and more of his time alone, at The Haunt.

Chapter XII

He Stumbles Onto the Bow

CARNACK commenced to inscribe his story on the rock when he had been resorting to The Haunt for about two years. So much, at least, we gather from internal and correlative evidence which it would be tedious to go into here.

At first, no doubt, his visits were infrequent. Sometimes days went by without him going there. Then, we must imagine, he begins to go there almost daily. Presently he begins to spend his nights there in pleasant weather. Next he builds a little shelter for himself in foul; a few branches leaned against the rock beneath his tree beside the spring; a branch at a time, added one by one when the rain keeps coming through; not yet even a hint of the hut that was to arise there.

He gives us pictures of the place at this time, deliberate views, apparently, telling us nothing but how beautiful it was, and how he loved it. In one of them, which is typical, a deer is drinking at the spring. It turns to look at him. A wolf is slink-

ing up the gulch at the head of the little valley.
Perhaps it is Loof. Possibly Carnack is intending
to tell us about Loof for the first time. We begin
to see this shaggy monarch of the pack in many of
the pictures now, lurking at a distance. This may
be the first time that Carnack has recognized and
identified his visitor; realized that it was the same
one coming back.

I have a strong impression that as time went on
Carnack ceased to kill game in The Haunt, or allow
others to—if he bothered to kill it anywhere, now
that the hunters from Shoulder Hill brought it to
Boulder Rock every day. If the picture of the deer
at the spring tells us anything at all, it tells us that
the animal is not afraid of Carnack. Similarly we
see rabbits and squirrels skipping happily about,
with now and then a bear. In one picture, much
later, of course, but still on the topic, Skihack is
running away from The Haunt, hunting spear in
hand, with an arrow dangling from his arm. Of
course his errand might have been another one than
poaching.

We have another reason, and a final one, for our
conclusion. If the thought of killing, with its
hatred and fear, had been present in The Haunt,
Loof would not have come there by slow degrees

into the intimacy and fearless friendship that came forth between these two. It was the very absence of this thought that compelled him there; and it was Loof's very fierceness, his own lust for killing, that drew him, of all the others, to that spot where the burden of his fierceness was removed from him; the fierceness that the Adam man had condemned him to and from which this son of God, exercising his right dominion over all of God's other creatures, released him, restoring him to his right identity and place beside the lamb.

We have several pictures of Carnack busy with his friends; squatting against the rock beneath the tree by the spring-side; picking up a nodule or a piece of one; turning it this way and that to study the planes of its cleavage; tossing it up and catching it as it comes twisting down, with his hammerstone in his other hand ready to begin; clicking it, cracking it, with his gaze fixed on the serrated edges of the cloven fragment; swiftly, with firm blows of precision, bringing out the shape that he wants.

Blish has taught him this; Blish the incompetent; Blish the unable; Blish the forerunner, ahead of his times without being big enough; uncommonly gifted; highly endowed with potentials of usefulness lost to himself and to others because nobody knew what was there, nobody saw how to use it, least of all Blish, born without fiber, fiery purpose, courage and confidence, selfless reliance, the hubbub of spirit that's needed.

We hear the strokes of the hammer-stone; the smack and the crash of the cleavage; the faint little "chick" of the tiniest pieces pressed off from the surface to bring out the texture; the "chick" as they strike on the ground that is covered with others; the purl of the brook; the soft, sandy sibilance of the spring-pool, whispering to itself; the rattle of leaves overhead; the wind in the grasses, the cry of a bird, a stir in the bushes.

Now and then he lays down his tools, tosses back his lank, hanging hair, and looks around. Looks down to the grass by the brook to see if a deer is there. Watches the leaves as they lift and tremble in the breeze. Finds a bird and watches it. Follows the heavy path of a bee from flower to flower, or homeward with its honey. Looks up the gulch for Loof; the wolf that keeps coming back alone. Listens to the brook, to the more distant rush of the waterfall and cascade. Loafs in the sun for a luxurious moment. Invites his soul—to what? Then, click, click, click, at another flint.

But flint making does not take all his time, and

loafing in the sun is not enough for this son of God. He strolls about; up the gulch; down by the water-fall; out along the brink of the precipice to the left, around the buttress of the little valley, to the bench beneath the tree, high perched on the cañon's brow.

He has been there before. It is one of his favorite spots. He likes to stand under the tree and look down into the cañon; down onto the tree tops, patterned in variant green; and saffron and yellow and red in the autumn; with the permanent, up-shafted emerald of pines. He likes to look off at the ridges from there—trace them out; trace them up to the peak ridge.

On a day he stands there looking out. Brimming afternoon; hot sparkle of sunlight through tree tops and rock ribs; bushes exhaling; upswinging pungency; the basin afloat in its heat haze; sharp edges dulling on distant declivities; an indolent eagle, poised in the azure; the rock at his back, aflush in the day-flood; shadow of tree-leaves dappling the ground.

He feels that he wants something. Something that the sunshine almost gives him; that the cool cañon's depths, the triumphant ridges, the sky, the trees, the far-off tilted plain of the basin, the air that fans him, the trees above him, hold out, but evade him with. Something that he cannot see, cannot hear, cannot clutch, cannot kill or catch. It is not the others at the cave. It is not Starga.

He picks up a piece of flat rock. He has a shard of flint in his hands; one that he brought with him, feeling its edges, turning it over and over absently. A pocket piece. A charm. Something to finger.

He scratches on the flat stone with the flint. A line. And another. Half a dozen more; aimlessly, almost; at random. He looks at them. He has drawn a face. A man. Old Huckar.

He looks for another piece of stone. He will try again; draw another; the rest of him this time. He sees the sheath of rock, smooth, inviting, clean, at the back of the bench. He goes over to it, noting well how smooth it is.

He begins on the flat face of it; draws out a figure; stands back and looks at it. Thrills at the sight of it. Awakens to something. Commences another.

Thus he begins.

And thus he continues; aimlessly at first, at odd places on the rock. We find these first pictures scattered everywhere, confusingly.

But by degrees a purpose and a plan. A beginning—and an end.

Meanwhile life was enriching him with other things.

He was working out the bow and arrow, and beginning on his hut.

The discovery of the bow is set forth in two exquisite little pictoliths, already spoken of.

In the first Carnack is seen stumbling over a vine hanging from a sapling. At the same moment a stick is observed flying through the air from the tree, fixed in the ground at a little distance, and still clinging tangled to the sapling. This is not the only time that Carnack traces a sequence of events by repetition of the same object in a single scene; a practice enormously confounding, like many others he employs, until seen through and understood, when it becomes equally enlightening.

The second picture of the pair discloses Carnack standing behind a sapling with a vine clinging to it from which he has just discharged a javelin and laid low a deer.

It is not difficult to weave a web from these two threads.

Carnack, on a day in the summer, is sitting in his nook beside the oak tree making spear shafts.

He has added this work to the chipping of flints for the others.

He finds himself in need of some straight, new growth to make his spear shafts of.

He knows where there is some; up the little gulch where the spring comes down.

He picks up a largish, flattish chunk of flint worked down into a sharp edge along one side which he has learned is good to hack down trees with— he has not yet learned to fix a handle to it—and starts out up the gulch, parting his way through the thick, dry brush at its mouth, churning the rocky soil of the steep ascent with his strong bare feet.

Higher up he comes to an open flat—a tiny one. It is still there. We came upon it ourselves, the boys and I, in some of our foolish, inconsequential explorations on our first visit.

Saplings grow here and there—slim, slender, springy trees. Young, but not too young for one of them to have a vigorous vine already climbing into its top, with a long trailing stem behind.

Carnack, intent upon his search for suitable spear shafts, trips in the vine.

It sends him lurching, but he is quick to catch himself.

He sees, as he recovers himself, a piece of dead limb hurtling over the tops of low bushes; observes it strike against the ground with force enough to make it stick there.

It has not fallen from a tree; he sees that.

Has someone thrown it?

He grasps his coup-de-poing and looks around.

The sapling is still swinging; the vine tautening and slackening.

Once as it snaps back it throws off a strand of loose bark, left by the stick. He goes over and picks up the stick. He remembers that he saw one like it fastened to the vine on the tree.

He goes back to the sapling.

The stick he saw in the vine is gone.

He looks at the one in his hand; the one that had flown through the air. It is the one he saw on the tree.

No doubt this young man, unshod, clad in skins, lank hair hanging in his eyes, thick lipped, with white, heavy teeth and hands smelling of a thousand deeds done with them, is perpetually bewildered by little things like this that happen to him; little glimpses into something that he cannot see. No doubt he stands there, immensely mystified, trying to figure out an occurrence that others would pass by unheeded—and would still be passing by, in skins and flints, if men like this one had not wondered at them.

He looks at the stick, looks at the tree with the vine on it, puts the stick back in the vine where he had seen it, walks off, comes on, stumbles over the vine again as he had done the first time, watches what happens, sees the stick fluttering off, whirling this time, perhaps.

What makes it go?

Why does it not go end on again, as it had done in the first instance?

What made it go end on before?

What if it should go end on every time?

What if it were a javelin, going end on like that?

With one of his keen, tapering, heavy-shouldered flints fastened to it?

He tries it again and again; breaks the stick; finds another one, with a tiny forking branch near its upper end; slips the vine into this fork; learns that it goes farther that way, and more nearly straight, end on.

The vine pulls away, overtaxed. He looks for another one like it; cannot find one; goes back and winds the first one on the tree again, and resumes his experiments—or his play.

We do not know, of course, the steps and stages

from that chance tree with a vagrant stick tangled in its vine to the lithe bow and slender arrow which we see him with eventually; all the cumbrous, obvious deductions he had to make along the way; all the long journeys round about which he took to learn things we know so easily, but a next step is shown quite clearly in the second picture.

He has rigged up a sapling in a runway where he knows the deer will come; has made a javelin with a fork on it like the stick that had one part way down; has chipped out a head for it and bound it into the slit end of the shaft with deer-thongs; and has slain his deer, by way of experiment and demonstration.

Amazing thing!

Amazing thing for this first thinker to accomplish. Back there at the awakening of time. Alone. Sprung from a people dumb beyond comprehension or comparison. Without a guide or prompter. With no one since the human species had emerged from chaos to tell him that there was anything to think or see; think about or look at. To grapple with the flying twig until he had wrung an answer from it.

As amazing as the telephone, the aeroplane, the submarine and radio, the locomotive and the print-

ing press. As amazing as Archimedes, Newton,
Franklin, Edison. As amazing as Hamlet and the
Gettysburg oration. Too amazing for Cassell, for
instance. Carnack, he says, could not have worked
out the bow. The bow, he claims, was introduced
from another tribe; brought in, perhaps, by Knumf
on his return.

There was another tribe, as we are to learn, and
Knumf undoubtedly did come in contact with them
while he was away; but they had no bows, and he
came back long after the bow was in Carnack's
hands. But it is not necessary to refute Cassell.
His repudiation of Carnack's bow merely illustrates
the shackles which too much learning can place upon
intelligence by restricting understanding of events
and men, to man's own puny, trumped-up catego-
ries which he calls natural laws, leaving out that
which alone accounts for the achiever and whatever
is achieved in human progress and unfoldment.
Leaving out the spirit working on and in the human
agent which is man's only natural law and which
makes him fetterless and free, unshackled by false
impositions that say it shall be thus and thus and
thus with him, and thus alone.

Upon what natural laws of men as men have writ
them out, what principles of personality or intel-

lect or inheritance or training, shall we account for the unschooled Shakespeare or the uncouth Lincoln, let us say, without filling up the page with more ancient prophets; the one uncovering human nature as no one since Jesus had uncovered it, the other breaking human bondage alike for slave and master with a liberating, healing love as no man since Jesus has? What manner of natural phenomena, as men call nature, are these two? Or any of the rest of us, for that matter, in so far as we, like them, unmask the false nature of mankind and bring out his true nature as the son of God, under His natural laws of wisdom and intelligence and truth and love and the graces of the spirit? What is amazing about Carnack, when we understand? What is amazing is that there were not more Carnacks, sooner, out on the plains of Utah, under God. That there is any lack of Carnacks now. That we should still be muddling about in our caves of war and poverty, disease and vice, unhappiness and discord.

The next step in the bow we arrive at by inference. Deer would not always come at convenient times to runways where he had rigged up his saplings and lay in wait for them. He must take his javelin hurler to them. This is simple; hacking off the stem of a young tree with flint axe and knife;

twisting a vine about one end; thrusting the other end into the ground, or holding it firm with his foot when he wishes to use it.

No doubt it is quite a while before he twists the free end of the vine about the free end of the sapling; before he learns that he need not rest the end of the bow on the ground. Longer still, perhaps, before he finds that a smaller sapling will do as well, that it gets better and stronger as it dries out, that a vine can be improved upon as a bowstring by a deerthong or sinew. We do not know. We get glimpses of these stages, but no record of them. But at last we see the bow as the double-ended, curved affair of medieval times and the modern savage state with a thong of hide stretched from one bending end to the other. And we see the arrows growing in succeeding pictoliths from the hand-thrown javelin, too heavy and clumsy and too badly balanced for the quick, light bow, to the slimmer, shorter, straighter and more delicate shaft with its finer head of flint of Carnack's workmanship; and we find the perfected head amongst other trophies of his skill and industry picked up in The Haunt.

What did the young Carnack do with his bow when he had made it?

Go trotting off to the caves to show and share it with them?

I do not think he did.

I do not think he realized what he had found, at first.

I think he merely kept it by him, working at it, improving it with that urge of accomplishment and prick of expectant curiosity which drove him always; learning better how to use it.

But on a day. . . .

It is springtime again. Carnack draws the buds and grass for us, and puts a bird in.

The bow is still the crude affair.

He sets out with it, and a sheaf of arrows, in his hand; from The Haunt, no doubt, though possibly The Cave.

He proceeds to the caves at Shoulder Hill.

He does not come there much now.

They see him approaching.

They draw off in groups. Blozzip. Skihack. Palupe. Heetow.

The women gather in the caves.

The children stop their squealing and vanish.

The others must have known that he had this thing; must have seen him use it; must have been mystified and terrified by it, crying and whistling

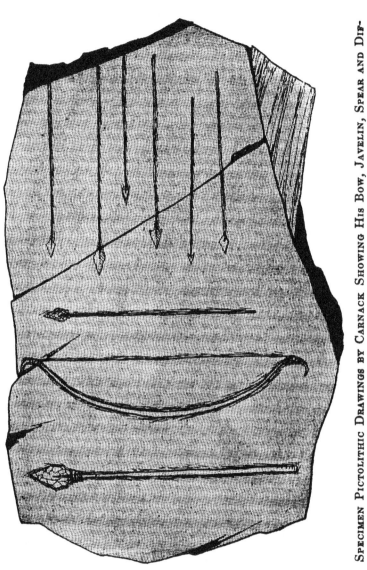

SPECIMEN PICTOLITHIC DRAWINGS BY CARNACK SHOWING HIS BOW, JAVELIN, SPEAR AND DIF-
FERENT SIZED ARROWS, ALL OF HIS OWN WORKMANSHIP. TROPHIES OF HIS SKILL
AND INDUSTRY PICKED UP IN THE HAUNT.

and killing from a distance. I am inclined at times to think that the bow and arrow was the first provocation of that dread and hatred of him that was to master them at last and drive him out, an exile; the first open challenge to the defensive life.

The sun has set in The Valley of The Caves. Carnack has chosen a time when all the hunters will be at home. The sharp line of the sunset shadow has climbed half way up the pink face of Shoulder Hill. The narrowing cañon above is suffused with blue dusk; the broad level of the valley, barely glimpsed, is aswim with the soft rose greys of coming mountain twilight.

Carnack stops. He fits an arrow, lifts his bow, pulls it, lets go, and a shaft, swifter than their sight is used to, stands trembling in the stout stem of an oak.

Old Huckar comes shambling down the slope, cautiously. Blozzip with more resolution.

Carnack lets go another shaft.

The men stand in their tracks; coming forward again, cautiously, in groups, supporting one another.

He holds out the bow and the arrows. It is here that the picture picks up the scene. Huckar sweeps them away with a gesture of scorn and of rage.

Blozzip takes hold of the bow, and hands it back quickly. Skihack looks at it slant-eyed. Heetow, of course, will have none of it, and sidles away, quicker than any to let that be known. Neither will Palupe. Nor Skook.

Thus Carnack offers the bow. And thus they refuse it, angry and terrified.

He gathers his arrows in silence, the men looking on; while the women watch from the cave mouths.

The children begin to reappear.

He turns into the path homeward.

A jabber breaks out in the circle behind him; a cackle of throat-clicks; muttering grunts; increasing as Carnack withdraws.

They shout and gesticulate as he goes down the path between the oaks; alone; back to the solitary cave on Boulder Rock.

Or to The Haunt.

Fading away through the dusk and the twilight.

Bearing his bow. And his arrows.

CARNACK HOLDS OUT THE BOW AND ARROWS. THE MEN
STAND IN THEIR TRACKS.

CHAPTER XIII

STARGA SEES THE HUNTERS GO BY

WHEREIN, in any worthy, comprehensive
sense of the term, is Carnack to be held a
life-bringer for his puny fumblings amongst this
lost race in the dusk of forgotten ages, accepting the
word as meaning anything at all and conceding that
this particular man was a contributor and prophet
to his times? Wherein did he bring life in any
larger and enduring sense to humanity? What is
there in world experience or human consciousness
today which we can point to as having sprung from
him?

We have no answer which we can ask the logician
or the man of business, the biologist, economist or
the person in the street, to accept. We cannot say,
for instance, that modern commerce, or the industrial machinery for distributing food which makes
organized society possible today, are lineal descendants of what befell this groping soul out amongst the
lonely caves of Utah twenty-five milleniums ago,
rending venison from Huckar and the others in
exchange for flints.

We cannot point to the loom or the printing press, the airplane or the automobile, as today's developments of mechanical principles which he noted and applied in the making of his bow and arrow. We cannot, in the smoke of our factories, in the throb of our locomotives crossing continents, in our steamboats pushing through the seven seas, in the cozy light and warmth of our modern caves high in our modern Shoulder Hills, find the glow and heat, the thrilling flame and illumination, of the tiny fire which he kindled and employed.

We cannot trace our flocks and herds, our animal companions and our beasts of burden, our butter and our milk supply, to his domestication of a wolf and horse; or our art and literature, our studies and accounts of man, to the shard of stone he pictured on the cañon wall. Our cathedrals and our country houses, our office buildings and our industrial plants of glass and steel, our apartment houses and our tenements, have not arisen from the rude hut which he threw up against his rock beside the spring.

We know how his people fought off these things. We know how they grew restive under his exactions of flesh they slew, albeit with his flints. We have seen them turn from his bow and arrow. We know what they would have done with Loof. We know, or are to learn, that when he brought them fire they drove him out. What the effect of his drawings was upon their enlightenment and aspiration we learn from a picture of this period, one of the most sinister and ominous, to me, amongst them all, in which we find Blozzip and Skihack—always Skihack—standing before the tablet of stone, half traced over by this time with the mysterious scratchings which they could not understand if they could read them, and see Blozzip lift and splinter his great club against them.

Even if Carnack's own reactions to enlightening experience did slowly mold and tincture his times and bend his people to a higher frame and hue of life, or if he did possibly become, as I have endeavored to suggest in a recent article in the *Prehistoric Review,* the remote Romulus of a departed, super-ancient Rome which is being now uncovered from Nevada's dust, no direct trace of his impulse has come down alive in this hemisphere, and the hypothesis advanced by some of his protagonists that his influence spread across continental bridges, since submerged, into India and Egypt, travels too rough and dry a road to be entered into as a popular excursion.

At the same time there are those who are beginning to feel that forward impulses and true spiritual experiences, once set afoot, reach the boundaries of time and space, and that Carnack's going into business in Seafar Basin, his working out his bow, his subduing a wolf, his producing fire, might easily suggest themselves as original ideas hundreds of years later and thousands of miles distant to men who could never have been aware of the existence of such a one as Carnack.

For man does not originate or create his own thoughts. He reflects, instead, ideas that have always been in Mind, receiving their impetus, focus, direction, as they impinge upon him; turning them to use; illuminating others with them; or letting them glance off and pass on until they reach a more worthy steward at another time. Nothing came to Carnack that Old Huckar might not have had.

The ideas of native Mind having once come to him, however, having once been grasped within the consciousness of his human mind, once gathered by him into sheaves of human experience, once brought within the compass and familiar knowledge of one of mankind, were thereby prepared and made forever after easier for other human minds to grasp and gather into usefulness. The way had been broken. The great gulf fixed by man between himself and God was bridged. The human spirit was no longer alone and without distinct experience to guide and encourage it toward truth.

We see concepts of the spirit growing thus amongst us today; leaping from one to another without personal communication; gathering momentum, widening the circle; silent, above impediment, resistence or interruption. We see it in the better thought of business, in the slow and steady pressing forward of the anti-sensual idea underlying prohibition, in the growing sentiment and hope for peace, in the mastery which ideals of brotherhood and helpfulness, promoted by no leader but given impetus by all who entertain them, are achieving over the imagination and the vision of the world.

In this unfolding reflection of individual ideas into universal human consciousness lies the hope of humanity; the healing of all its diseases, the wiping away of its tears, the true forgiveness of its sins in the destruction of them; salvation and eternal life; for it is the same will of God that works thus in us. "My words shall not pass away," said the author and finisher of this faith who never wrote a line— save once, in the dust—but was himself the Word made flesh to dwell amongst us, and who, above all others and all else, worked out the will of God on earth which we see slowly stirring Carnack, away back there in the corridors of time. To those who see him thus Carnack is seen to be a life-bringer for all time, breaking through the arid and unplowed plateaus of human ignorance, a weary way for all of us which never can be lost.

Carnack, of course, was not aware of anything like this as he wound his way homeward down the path that night leaving the cackle and clatter behind him to fade away in the dusk and the twilight and distance. It was far from his thoughts as he stalked up the step to the rock top, flinging his bow in a corner and pawing around for a morsel of meat before turning in to the nest; or emerged from the last climb past the waterfall on to the little high-perched flat and sought out the nook, leaning his bow on a tree and crawling into his hut in the dark. No doubt he was wondering and mystified, and somewhat disappointed; perhaps even angry and resentful. But nothing more than that. There were many things about his people now that confused and baffled him, and this was merely one of them.

The hut which we begin at this period to find in The Haunt followed, as a consequence, I think, the bow and arrow. Carnack's new weapon made it easier for him to hunt his own food than to go to Boulder Rock for a supply, and this made it unnecessary for him to go there at all except for shelter. So he built himself a shelter where he preferred to be; developed his silly little lean-to into something more adequate.

It was a rough affair. Any boy could build a better one today. Little more than a wattle of branches daubed over with mud and patched out with rushes and reeds brought up from the lake, miles away; an armful, no doubt, on each trip when he comes by empty-handed. At least we have a little sketch of him gathering them there, and find them put to no other use. Probably he found long-withed willows in the cañon beneath the waterfall. No doubt he used fir and hemlock and spruce boughs.

At the same time he employed masonry of the crudest sort; rough stones found lying around or pulled out of the bank and laid up into a loose wall two or three feet high. He may have blocked these stones around the ends of his wattles to hold them in place. It would have been an obvious thing to do, and the ground, at the present time, at least, is too hard to have allowed him to thrust the ends of the brush walls into it far enough to keep them fixed.

In the same way we find him laying up rocks across the entrance to the family cave on Boulder Rock at about this time; a sheltering partition no doubt suggested both by the winter snowdrift that formed there every year and by what he was doing in The Haunt; although the cave partition may have antedated and led to the hut. In any case, in the following winter, which he pictures as a hard one, we find it full blown and in use.

The roof of the hut quite clearly gave him difficulties. He made it out of boughs and rushes, to all appearances, laid on thickly, but without support. I have no idea that it kept the rain out, even when the leaves were green and the stems of the rushes fresh, and more than once it must have come tumbling in upon him.

The affair was very small, barely large enough for him to crawl into and squat down in; very dark, with only one small opening next the rock to enter through; and, by the same token, unquestionably very foul. Nevertheless it was a structure of the first importance to mankind, for it was a habitation made by hand and one that could be put up anywhere; and man, theretofore locked within the rigid limits of his cave with no alternative but precarious refuge from the weather and the beasts in trees and bushes and what holes he could burrow in the ground, was henceforth free to go where fancy or the pursuit of food might call him.

Fischer insists that the hut was not an innovation introduced by Carnack, but that his people had long been using it habitually in the summer time, when they left their caves and went on long hunting campaigns into distant regions, taking their women and children with them. He found, in the open country within range of the district, remains of prehistoric camps which he says prove this—middens of bones and broken flints and other signs.

There is nothing in these ancient middens to date them before Carnack's hut; but, on the contrary, much to show that they were of a later period. What they do prove to me is that Carnack's discovery or invention of the hut brought his people, long afterward, when they had by slow marches of the spirit adopted and adapted it, the freedom to move about in richer, unexhausted regions which became a life and death necessity with them when the pressure of expanding population against the inelastic resources of the caves and the diminishing supply of food animals made sociology and economics too difficult within the limitations of The Valley of The Caves.

Why the problem of increasing numbers had not become acute in Carnack's time I do not know. Fischer, before he found his middens, solved it to his satisfaction in migration and the picture of Blish at the pool with a baby in his hands. The size of Blish's family, as we have said, disposes of the latter argument. If any cave had need of depopulation his had. If there was migration Carnack fails to tell us of it. His own departure from the country was not that. Cassell informs me, rather surprisingly, that the families of savages are not large, even with a multiplicity of mothers. Blish's facile fatherhood, he maintains, is almost if not quite unique. This, with normal diminution due to hunger and privation and exposure and predacious beasts and the fortunes of the chase would keep the population question under more or less control without huts or emigration or infanticide.

Carnack, of course, has to forego his hut in the wintertime. His first one, at least. We see him building a second one, later on, which could withstand the snows and keep out the cold as well as a cave and no doubt better, being smaller and far less open, and with a low ceiling. Then came fire, and made life possible at any point. But the first one he abandons when the weather closes in, leaving The Haunt itself, no doubt, until spring, with perhaps a visit to it in pleasant open weather when the drifts are not too deep on the northern slopes and in the cañons.

The winter turns out to be a heavy one. The storms are long and savage, he shows us, with bitter winds. The hunters from the caves come back empty-handed. He fares better with his bow. He can bag the wild beasts with it from beyond the circle of their fear of man, accustomed as they are to the short-range javelin and throwing stick. We see him bringing down a moose in the grassy plain at the lower end of the lake; a valiant shot, if we may judge of the distance from Carnack's primitive perspective.

Domestic matters at the cave have undergone a change, apparently, since he began to spend so much time at The Haunt. Most of the nameless ones have disappeared; amongst them, if I am not mistaken, the one against whom Carnack had felt called upon to assert the doctrine of self-determination with a bison bone. Whether he has plied the bison bone too often or too well, or whether the object of his instructions has found a more congenial and appreciative atmosphere elsewhere, is not vouchsafed us.

Moox, I am afraid, has been ruined by prosperity. She is clearly getting lazy. Laa'aa and Starga dress the skins and the meat that Carnack brings in, while she sits at the bottom of the cave, staring and waiting. What she is waiting for is not apparent. It is not likely that she is waiting for anything except to be hungry again, or sleepy, or for the sun to come out so that she can move onto the top of the rock once more and wait there, basking in its warmth.

Laa'aa has not mated yet. I have never understood this. It is far past her time. She may have been lacking in charm, and without a dejected and despairing Blish to be contented with her, or she may have remained single by election. For it is not to be decisively assumed from the adventure which we have witnessed descending upon the provocative Teltob or from Starga's experience with the nameless one, or from that other stray and pointless picture to which so many point as proof of this or that, in which we perceive a young man in full cry after a young woman with much attendant excitement on the part of both, that the young women of the time were wooed without alternative. No doubt an object of particular desire encountered by an admirer unaccompanied and far from home found the situation less difficult if she could contribute willingness, or at least passive acquiescence, to his advances and go meekly with him to his den. It is possible that this last picture is a ballad in the classic mode celebrating poetically and in a general way such a romance; unless, as some suggest, it is reminiscent of an affair of Carnack's, a fleeting fancy which came to nothing; for the young man is not unlike him. But this or nothing else in the records compels us to believe in the actual invasion of a cave and open abduction of a reluctant daughter of the rocks as the only form of courtship. So Laa'aa might have been celibate from choice.

Not so Starga. Starga, we are soon to see, has thrilled long enough in vain to her sense of Carnack; his smooth, swart skin, his muscular movement, his stride and his gesture, his vigorous sinewy body, the sound of his voice, the soft, springy hair on his breast, the hair on his forearm and thigh and the calf of his leg. No more will she await his return from the hills with brimming heart, as she did in the days before he went so much to his hiding place above the waterfall; watching him with glowing eyes as he approached, deer slung over shoulder, her brother Inkin at his heels; running to meet him; taking the kill from his shoulder; helping him with it, gazing at him as they ate; curling close to him in the nest. Sad and wistful at first, perhaps, when he began to be away so much, missing his goings and his comings, the sound of his voice, the feel of him amongst them. It is not hard for us to imagine the smouldering hurt and resentment that came into her breast, the stolid, morose rebellion, the lifting of the eyes elsewhere.

Spring comes at last, suddenly, with a warm abundance that makes amends for the long, hard winter; swelling in the buds, singing in the brooks, rushing through the land, spreading it with green, embracing all her children in her soft arms, caressing them with redolent and balmy breath, weeping over them with overflowing heart. The air is alive with the light and the lilt of her; the singing of birds; the color and fragrance of flowers. And Starga is strangely exuberant—strangely astir and aloof from young Carnack.

Carnack gets ready to set out for The Haunt. He has brought in enough game, left flints for Inkin to bargain with. Why should he wait any longer.

He is eager, unhappy, disturbed. He stands on

the rock looking westward. He gives us the picture. The sun fills the valley. The trees are washed clean. The herbage is tender. A breeze fans his cheek. Something embracing exhales from the earth and the air, the sky and the rocks; creeps over him, into him.

The shouting of the hunters from The Caves reaches Boulder Rock. They are coming down the trail toward The Basin.

The din increases, approaches; a tumult of yells, shrill, and hoarse. Like the screaming and neighing of stallions, the bellow of bison bulls, the low of the bison cows. Like the crest of a river in cloudburst, rushing down in a clamorous torrent.

Starga runs into the cave and comes out again. Not often do the cave men work themselves up like this for the hunting. She is deliciously stirred and excited—ecstaticly frightened.

They file into view in the field, wading through the grass, stamping and leaping, waving their arms, crooking their bodies, clashing their weapons together.

Blozzip, huge and vigorous, hairy, thundering, shaking the earth with his feet, comes at the head of them, flashing his eye.

Starga crouches down on the rock.

Behind him come Skihack and Palupe and Skook —mighty ones all, men of affairs. Life in the cave at its best. Out on the hunt. Coming back soon with the spoils of their prowess. Fresh flesh. Skins to be dressed and put on. Huckar trots after them. Something has happened that Blozzip should lead—something exciting.

Inkin picks up his spear and his javelin.

The hunters swing into the pines, Blozzip gleaming before them; naked bodies, flapping hides, bristling spears, passing by in flashes caught behind the pine boles, now seen, now eclipsed.

Starga runs into the cave and comes out again. She half closes her eyes at times. Something catches her breath, something thumps in her throat.

Inkin leaps down the path-steps from the top of the rock; hides himself in the bushes; pushes out; squats and watches, holding his spear on the ground; terrified, charmed.

The hunters emerge from the pines and strike off down the valley.

Moox gives a faint, lazy laugh. Her dry little eyes glow for a moment, and moisten, with a dull, old fire. It passes, slowly, as it came; and she continues to stare at what she was staring at when it began.

Inkin runs down the trail after the hunters.

Starga sinks onto the rock and remains there, watching the hunters dwindle and vanish.

Now and then they hear a shout down by the lake.

Carnack loiters and lingers. He looks over his shoulder at Starga, watching, and picking out distant voices. He looks over at Moox, staring obscenely. Gazes at Starga.

Uncertain, reluctant, he takes a step toward her, stands by her, looks at her, clucks to her something . . . Goes off to The Haunt. Swings down through the pines and strikes out.

Starga's eyes follow him, mistily, absently. She runs into the cave.

The river is booming and lush near the lake. Carnack has to ascend it to cross it. Plover wheel from the margins; ducks arise with a clatter. He carries his bow at his side, slung over his shoulder.

He expands, as he goes, to the season. He quickens his pace. He flies up the ridges. The trail is obscure, beaten flat, washed away, cluttered in places with boulders and rock slides. He finds it, or traces another. Birds and bees . . . Flowers . . . Young leaves on the trees . . . Ferns in the cañons, unrolling . . . Cataracts shouting . . .

Grassy plots springy with rain-juice . . . Flowers
and bees . . . The sun over all . . . And the soft,
tender breeze . . .

The green, gentle bed of The Haunt as he stands
at its threshold, drinking it in, breathing the air of
it. The fresh, clean rocks, the trees asparkle with
new leaves, the brook running through. The deer
grazing in it; antelope, elk.

He unslings his bow and fits in an arrow; puts it
down; does not shoot.

The animals eye him; scamper off as he enters;
at leisure, looking back; standing still now and
then; talking it over.

He goes to his nook. The spring leaps to see
him. Folds of its water reach after him. The tree
stoops in the breeze to caress him. He flings down
his bow and his arrows.

The hut has caved in. It is only a tangle of
branches and rushes.

Pieces of flint lie around; split-up nodules; half-
finished spear heads.

Something has been in his hut; made a den of it
throughout the winter; working it into a nest again
after it had fallen. Clearly a wolf. A sniff tells
him that. The one he has seen there so much?
Bigger and fiercer than any? But harmless to him?

He picks up a flint. Looks around, at the trees, up the gulch, down the vale.

He wanders down to the creek and watches it scamper over its oozy bed, heaving and leaping, hurrying down to the waterfall.

He follows it down and stands at the head of the cataract, gazing down into the cañon; off toward the lake, and the valley where the caves are.

He goes out to his bench; inspects the last picture; the one that fall interrupted. He recalls it and builds it up again in his thoughts; picks up a graving tool and a hammer-stone and makes a few lines.

He goes back to the nook and looks at the ruins of his hut.

On the way he sees the wolf up the gulch and waves an arm at him. The wolf lopes off, turning to look now and then, and to sit on his haunches; lifting his head at the last in a howl, which Carnack replies to.

Carnack stirs the ruins of his hut with his foot, kicking it apart. He picks out some of the branches and starts to build it up again.

The leaves fall off. The rushes are cracked and split and lifeless.

He goes off up the gulch where the wolf disappeared, uttering the wolf-call.

He returns to the nook and picks up his coupde-poing to cut some fresh branches with; spruce, with their flat-lying needles.

He starts up the ridge where he knows some are growing, but comes back without them.

He goes out to the bench again; looks at his pictures; gazes over the mountains.

Returns, and begins work on a spearhead.

Tinkers with his hut.

Moves about.

The sun goes away from his rock. It leaves the little valley, climbing the walls of it with a ruddy, brimming trace. Shadows creep in and gather. The birds twitter in the trees, settle down. Dusk comes. It grows dark.

Carnack tears off a handful of flesh from the piece he brought with him and eats it, twisting his head; stopping to swallow.

He scoops up a drink, looks around, looks up at the stars, and crawls under the boughs next the rock, pulling them over him. In the morning he will build up the hut.

He draws his skins around him, curls up, falls asleep, his head on his arm; naked elbow on the harsh earth; protected from the wild beasts of the field and forest by the protection that he gives them there.

The hushes of the night deepen over him. The scintillating stars look down.

Now and then the muttering rumble of unseen, far-off Grash-po-Nash wells up through the pleasant, hissing rustle of the water-fall, the contented gossip of the brook, the whisper of the spring, the soft foot-steps of the night wind.

In the night the wolf calls in the gulch, and Carnack answers it. Twice it calls, and he twice.

And so, the morn.

All this, of course, is sheerest gossamer. We have not a picture for it.

But there is Carnack, and The Haunt, and the flints we have held in our hands, and the rockful of pictoliths, and the wolf-dog. These things we know. They must have come about in some manner. He lived in The Haunt; went to it; wrought there; found Loof there. How, if not in some such way as this?

CHAPTER XIV

"CAVE LIFE AT ITS BEST"

CONCERNING Loof, Carnack now becomes
more definite. This is the point in the record
at which he begins to tell us directly about him.
The wolf ceases to be an incident in scattered scenes
and becomes so much the center of all of them that
some commentators on the pictoliths maintain that
Carnack's prime purpose in them was to tell the
story of his dog.

In one picture which we soon come to Loof is
clearly a deliberate visitor, surprising Carnack at
his work beside the spring. The wolf has come
down the little side gulch which comes out at the
spring. He stands stiff-legged, bristling, ears
cocked. The notch in one of them by which we
came at first to know and identify him is in evidence. He was aware, from the whiff he got of
Carnack and the clicking of the flints, that Carnack
was there. Nevertheless he came and stood looking.

Shortly, we find Loof sitting on his haunches at
a distance—not too great a one—watching Car-

nack. Other visits no doubt have intervened. This one merely marks a stage; hence the drawing of it. It has no other meaning, no bearing on events. The animal is merely sitting there, quietly, jaws slightly apart, weighing matters.

We next observe him lying, we might say, at Carnack's feet; just across the spring-pool from him, hind legs twisted to one side, like a dog's, front paws extended in front of him toward Carnack, head erect, gazing at the man and comfortably panting in the sun. Carnack has thrown him meat, undoubtedly brought from the cave on Boulder Rock for the purpose or slain on the way with the bow, but Loof has had enough.

In a few days—or weeks—we find him curled up at Carnack's side, chin on paws, reposeful and content. And presently we see him following Carnack, as a matter of course, into the hills, going with him down to Seafar Basin, sitting by him while he fishes in the streams and lakes, trotting at his heels, apparently, as far as the cluster of pines in front of Boulder Rock when Carnack returns to the cave, or going there to wait for him, for we see him sitting expectantly on his haunches amongst the yellow stems in one picture Carnack gives us of him at this time. No doubt they had a call for each other; some cry of the pack that Carnack picks up.

How far the wolf surrenders to him, whether Carnack lays his hand on him, or offers to, how much control the man has over him, we are not told. I can imagine that the animal still maintains a wild, fierce freedom. Later, Carnack can command him within limits, and quiet his excitement.

All this time their meetings and companionship are cautious and clandestine. Loof draws the line at Carnack, as we are told in a pictolith in which we detect him peeping out upon the man through the bushes at the mouth of the little gulch on an occasion when Inkin has accompanied Carnack to The Haunt. We catch sight, between the leaves, of the burning eyes and the ear with a notch in it. Inkin, apparently, is not so observant. Loof remains a secret from everyone until the friendship is revealed to the community in a dramatic and exciting manner, as we are to see.

The scientific experts, almost to a man, grew prodigiously excited over this account of Carnack's friendship with the wolf which they saw unfold before their very eyes, the first recorded and only authentic instance of man's original domestication of an animal. They fall at odds beyond the threshold of that fact, but so far they go hand in hand, indulging in much felicitation back and forth over the "material", before their unanimous satisfaction in its discovery gives place to differences over what to make of it.

Its significance, however, I have always felt, lies much deeper than they see it. What was between these two, it seems to me, was not an accidental foregathering of a man of the caves and a beast of field and forest, brought about by chance and circumstance and advanced by bribes of meat on the one hand and assistance in the hunt on the other, as the scientists suggest, but was in essence and effect that true dominion over every living thing which is revealed to us in the first chapter of Genesis as a quality and gift of God, Himself possessed by His image, man. In seeing gentleness and fidelity, affection and response, trustfulness and trustworthiness in the wolf, Carnack, through the will of God that was at work in him, was seeing the wolf as God conceived it and as Isaiah beheld it dwelling with the lamb, and not as Adam, drowsing off into his dream of material sense, had named this idea at random and in ignorance when called upon to ascribe some name to it. This correct understanding of this living thing not only blessed Loof with true freedom, but also

Carnack himself with the abundant, joyous sense of God which was his own birthright. In reflecting toward Loof the love and intelligence of God he became conscious, however hazily, of God Himself.

It would not be surprising if in this consciousness Carnack found what seemed to him an answer, nebulous enough, to be sure, inarticulate and incoherent, but nevertheless an answer, to the hounding quest and query in him which no other experience had so far given back; a faint, far-off prophecy and promise of something that he hoped and hungered for which nothing else and no other person— neither the stars, the flowers, nor the winds, the solitary cañons, majestic mountain tops nor chattering streams, The Haunt, The Valley, The Basin nor The Lake, sunset nor noonday, midnight nor sunrise, storm, nor moonlight; Blish, beforetime, with his hovering confusion, Inkin, with his pottering imitativeness, Starga, with her large-eyed gaze, Laa'aa, with her meaningless light heart, Old Huckar, with his four fat wives, Blozzip, Skihack, Heetow nor the rest, nor the gods of his people, if they had any—had been able to hold out to him.

Nor need it be surprising if the satisfying sense of life which Carnack gained by this breaking through into the realities confused itself in his thought with the animal itself; with the object that had evoked in him that quality of God which made him, without knowing it, of course, feel God. It does not follow, as some suggest, that he deified Loof in any way or viewed him as supernatural; but we can understand, I think, how his attachment for the wolf became deep and searching and inspiring, and how Carnack was led to place an emphasis upon the animal in his records out of all proportion to other achievements in his career as we appreciate them.

What did the people at the caves think, by this time, of the young Carnack; of his walking so much by himself, of his going about amongst them alone, of his wandering off for days at a time to the little flat perched high above a waterfall on a distant cañon's brow? What did they think of his hut, of his hewing away at a rock, making meaningless, unheard-of lines on it? They must have known of his tablet of stone. Why did they not efface it and destroy his work in forthright superstitious terror?

Because, I think, terror had not risen in them yet to the breaking point. We know that they must have been in awe of him and hated him in proportion to their dread, for hate is fear, and fear is hate.

But the defensive life was slow. It had not before been challenged. It aroused itself to danger sluggishly.

They still counted him amongst them, apparently. We see them all coming in a body to The Haunt to recruit him for a hunting expedition, I have always thought, for they are all armed for the chase—spears, javelins, knives, clubs. Perhaps they want his bow along; they may have accepted it thus far. We recognize Huckar, Blozzip, Palupe, Heetow, Skook, Skihack. They stand around him, back to the rock by the spring in the nook. Skihack, apparently, is the spokesman. We see him assuming that capacity more and more. Blozzip is backing him up. Skihack the diplomat, negotiator; Blozzip the big stick behind.

Carnack seems stubborn. It may be he complies with their request, whatever it may be, offers them his bow, but will not go himself, if that is what they have come for. There is no connected sequel to the scene, so far as we can tell. Do they go off up the gulch, down the cañon, complaining about him, crowding together, shouting louder and louder as they draw farther away? Or are they too simple-hearted yet for that? There is nothing in the picture, or those near it, that can tell us; no clue; no hint.

He goes to the caves at Shoulder Rock, we know, with flints and spears. He makes the completed product now, shaft and all, as we learn from scenes in which we find him doing it. They still give him flesh and skins, apparently, for he hunts very little for himself, and that little only casually, on the way to and from The Haunt, knocking over with his bow and arrow stray game he comes across. They come to him at Boulder Rock, giving orders, accepting delivery, making payment.

At the same time I begin to think that he did not find his transactions with them any too agreeable. I can believe that he approached the caves at Shoulder Hill with caution, and considered it discreet to make wide detours when he met a hunting party in the trails, and to walk with circumspection through the tall grass by the lake and amongst the bushes on the foothills and the rocks that flanked his path.

Skihack with the arrow in his arm suggests another possibility. Have they begun to spy upon him? Has Skihack stolen up to see what practices keep this young man secreted so much of the time on the little valley shelf? Does Carnack detect him

and send him home with the shaft from his bow?
I have never accepted this. Such prowling would
have taught them sooner of his use of fire, and they
would have discovered Loof, almost certainly, before they did. Although Loof might have taken
care of that.   ,

That same summer Carnack makes his first expedition into Volcano Basin; Loof with him.
What does he go for? Men do not, as a rule,
travel there alone. It is too wide a place; too wild.
Does he go to confront the tribal gods in Grash-po-
Nash? Blish no doubt has told him about them,
with interpolations of his own, perhaps. Blish, I
can imagine, was not entirely orthodox in spiritual
matters. He was not quite sure of everything
others told him. He was born, I have often
thought, ten or twenty thousand years before his
time and did not know what to do about it. One
of the things he did about it, I am afraid, was to
impart his perplexities and doubts and confusions
in a bemused and wistful way to Carnack, not so
much, I suspect, for the edification and benefit of
the boy as in an effort to work things out more
clearly for himself. Talking them over with Moox
was out of the question. Or with Skihack, his first
born. Or with Old Huckar. So I let myself be-

lieve that he rambled on to Carnack, and that Carnack listened to the mumble of a thought that Blish was trying to bring forth. Was Carnack out here now, in this lonely basin, given over to the mighty Grash-po-Nash, to see for himself what these gods were like that had puzzled Blish; to resolve his father's doubts, and his own?

We see him standing on the brink of the crater steadfastly looking into it. He draws the smoke for us, and attempts the flames with a few gashes in the rock.

The heat comes to him as he stands there. It is like the sun on a summer's day, he can feel; or like that thing that they sometimes see when a bright spear comes down out of the windy sky and rain, when the sun is covered up, with a tremendous shout and disappears, shaft and all, into a tree, and the tree tosses and dances and leaps away. And the cloud that comes up from the dancing tree is the same; yet not the same. It has a different taste.

We see him standing there with his bow, shouting to this mighty hunter that flings his spears through the sky. Is it the same hunter that rides through the day and leaves the sky spattered with spear points behind him?

Loof is uneasy at his heels.

Carnack lifts his bow, fits an arrow, draws, and lets it go in a long arc into the seething pit.

It strikes. There is a flash. It disappears. The pit is as it was; as he tries to show it; cloudy, and with flashes in it.

Is this his errand there?

The trip is difficult and hazardous. Waterholes are hard to find and far between. Carnack does not know where they are. He has to follow instinct and judgment, and what tracks of animals he comes across leading to them. He depends upon the waterholes for his food as well as water; for there are always animals near by at night and in the morning.

It is at such a waterhole, where a river breaks through to the surface, once at sundown, that we get our first glimpse of Pono. Carnack shows the setting sun and the wide expanse of plain and mountain rim with an amazing fidelity.

Carnack and Loof are approaching it stealthily, in the hope of food, taking advantage of the bushes and of the wind, if there is one at that hour. Carnack had a javelin and a spear, as well as a club and his bow and many arrows, for he is far beyond the reach of familiar material with which to renew his supply of weapons. Loof, who no doubt has learned well how to hunt with him by this time, is close at his heels.

A band of horses is drinking at the waterhole. Carnack strikes one down; a mare with a foal. The others run away, but the colt remains with its mother. Loof would have slain it, but Carnack restrains him. So the wolf-dog falls on the mother.

For three days, or possibly more—Carnack indicates the interval with three suns, but it may easily be that he could not count beyond one and the three are simply to indicate many—for three days the little beastie trots along with them; more or less at a distance, but still in their company; Loof, whether under durance or through understanding, accepting the strange companionship. The animal, of course, must have been able to browse for itself. Finally they come to another band of horses, or more probably the same one, and it skips off to them, Carnack evidently creating for it the opportunity to do so by creeping up close enough to the herd unobserved for the colt to attach itself to them.

He tells us this in seven scenes, very small, scattered about and rather cramped, tucked here and there into the pictoliths in a way that makes one certain that their insertion with such particularity was an afterthought; that he put them in long after the event when the sequel to it, transpiring on another momentous expedition into Volcano Basin which we are to learn about, gave it an importance which it did not have at first. For the little animal, I am convinced, was Pono; Pono the horse that came to him; man's first beast of burden; original servant; here seen as a colt.

It was while Carnack was away on this expedition that Knumf came back from his long absence, bringing with him a strange woman and their papoose and bearing tales, as well as he could convey them with loud excited gutterals and much pointing to the hills toward Grash-po-Nash and at his wife, of another people over there beyond many mountains amongst whom he has been all these years and whence he had brought this mate.

It is possible that Knumf came back before Carnack left. Some maintain, amongst them Cassell, on evidence which seems to me rather frail, that Carnack's journey into Volcano Basin was an exploration of the country inspired and stimulated by the stories Knumf brought back about it. The point, however, seems a petty one. It is enough that Knumf comes back, and that his return creates a flurry, apparently, both in the home cave and out of it. Carnack gives us the event; Knumf climbing

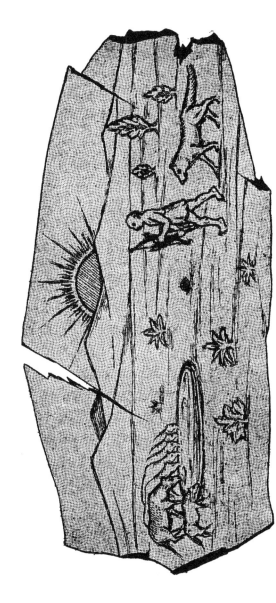

CARNACK AND LOOF ARE APPROACHING THE WATERHOLE STEALTHILY. CARNACK HAD A JAVELIN AND A SPEAR, AS WELL AS A CLUB AND HIS BOW AND ARROWS. THE SETTING SUN AND THE WIDE EXPANSE OF PLAIN AND MOUNTAIN AND MOUNTAIN RIM ARE SHOWN WITH AMAZING FIDELITY.

the path up Boulder Rock, wife and papoose at his heels, with the air and effect of a conscious hero. The family awaits him in surprise and awe. Carnack is missing; one of the reasons I find for believing that he was in Volcano Basin at the time. He puts this down from hearsay afterward and—stupendous thing!—his own dramatic imagination.

Carnack also shows Knumf squatting in the center of a circle of the mighty men and hunters at Shoulder Hill holding forth in clucks and pantomime for the benefit of the astonished stay-at-homes, while women fringe the group—an unprecedented circumstance—and children try to peep in between the knees and elbows of their elders for a better view of the amazing one.

Insofar as such highly descriptive epithets can be applied to a member of a group of human beings as dumb, on the whole, as the cattle in the field, Knumf, in comparison with the others, was quite debonair; a gay and vital fellow, attractive to the ladies, as we may infer from his bringing home a new bride from the Hill to Shoulder Rock on his second trip to the community, and popular with the men; suggestive and magnetic in his irresponsible, bubbling ways; a reckless harum-scarum who followed the bent of the moment even when it led him leagues across mountains and basins into strange countries, or deep into the heart of some neighboring cave group for a desire of the hour.

He appears, in his casual, careless way, to have been on pretty good terms with Carnack, and did him a good turn later on. We find him presently trading Carnack's flints for him—they must have been Carnack's; Knumf himself was never known to make one—in Inkin's place, for flesh and fowl. It is just possible that Knumf stole the flints from Inkin, and that Carnack got neither flesh nor fowl for them; but those in the nest did, which still kept them off Carnack's hands, so no doubt he was content. It seems probable that Knumf for a time drove quite a thriving trade in Carnack's goods, thereby releasing himself from the bother of hunting and conserving his time and attention for his new bride; but eventually it dwindled away, either because he grew tired of his business and neglected it, or grew tired of his bride and preferred to hunt again.

Starga is no longer in the cave.

We are not told precisely when she leaves, or the circumstances of her going.

But I think we may conclude that it was early in the spring.

We have been missing her from the pictures since that time.

That, of course, is not conclusive evidence. Not all of the family are in all the pictures of the home. They come and go.

It is not, however, until after Knumf returns that we find where she has gone.

We first see her again in the circle of women behind the circle of men at Shoulder Hill listening to this prehistoric Gulliver, this original Munchausen.

Presently we discover her in Blozzip's cave.

The surge of the spring that we saw in her, her disappointed lingering for Carnack, has been too much for her.

She has fallen to the mighty ones; embraced success; cave life at its best. The Eve in her has answered to the Adam call. Rib formed in a dream, and dreamed of still. Unawakened womanhood without meaning to awakened man. Awakened man without meaning, yet, to her. Instead, Blozzip of the mighty thew and curly hair and voice that rumbles in his chest; teeth that can tear, arms that can crush, hands that can slay, legs that can thrust back the scattering earth, eyes that can burn like Old Huckar's.

Blozzip is the leader now. He and Skihack have tapped Old Huckar on the head for the last time and Blozzip has taken his place. I am not sure that Old Huckar's sun did not begin to set on the day when Carnack gave him that click from behind a rock and took the dead deer away from him. It was the first crumbling stroke. Carnack showed them that Huckar was human like the rest of them; that their fear of him dwelt in themselves, not him. He showed again, as he had revealed when he stood upon his father's rock a naked lad, that the terrible eye of Old Huckar and the roar that shook the caverns to their depths in Shoulder Hill meant only what one let them mean.

Skihack, I think, was behind the final blow of Blozzip's club that did for Old Huckar as their chief man. Did for him morally, that is. His health is not heavily affected. I do not think that Blozzip would have thought of it without the other at his elbow. Skihack had evidently taken a leaf from his father's book of life when rather young and read his own lesson from the other side of it, as sons often do reverse the examples of their fathers, profiting by their senior's mistakes in one direction to make fresh ones of their own in another.

We have seen him at Blozzip's elbow from the

time they hunted together when Carnack was crawling around the parental cave looking for bugs and bones on top of Boulder Rock. We have seen him with Blozzip in the pine trees before The Rock, clicking Carnack; seen him stalking up the valley at Blozzip's heels, past Carnack in the bushes by the riverside, carrying a horse that they have killed; seen him fighting home through the blizzard with The Hairy One; setting up in a corner of his cave. We have seen him at the councils of the cave; seen him spokesman for them all up at The Haunt when they came after Carnack; seen, it seems to me, something adroit and sinister about him from the very first, working out the ways of evil with somewhat the same opening of intelligence that we see in Carnack, responsive to creative good. So it is not hard, I feel, to see his face behind Blozzip's elbow when the deposing club descends on Huckar's head.

It came about, I take it, in the spring of this very year. Winter has broken up and the time has come, or is approaching, for a foray in force into the basin. The men begin to shout about it from cave to cave, or when they meet each other coming home from little hunts into the hills, pressed against the receding snowline. They try out their javelins and spears in the cool dusk of evening, before their caves, hefting them, swinging them, thrusting with them. They balance their clubs in their hands, thinking of bison or horses. They mutter and mumble, growing excited. They gather together in groups, bringing their spears, showing each other how they use them, shouting and stamping and waving their arms. The women look on from the cave mouths; the children run to each other in silence, wide-eyed. The shouting goes on, and the tramping; the swinging of spears and the swaying of bodies; eyes are alight with thoughts of the chase, of past achievements and future successes. Their chests heave, their breath grates in their throats. They howl and shriek. Huckar comes down from his cave; Blozzip and Skihack. Night after night the performance repeats itself.

At last, on a morning, they start. No one has said to; no one has planned it. But Skihack and Blozzip loiter, as the others set out for the day's hunt, in the stamping ground. The breeze blows in warm from the basin; the sunlight floats soft in the feathery leafbuds. Skihack lifts up his javelin, shakes his arm, stamps, bellows; Blozzip echoes him. Palupe comes up, followed by Skook. They strike their weapons together, stamp and shout.

Skihack points to the sun in the trees, lifts his nose to the breeze, points down toward the basin, utters the scream of a horse in its death-cries. Old Huckar comes forth. And the others. Some turn back from their little excursions and arrive on the run, trailing weapons and shouting. The children flock out and stream through the trees, chasing each other, stopping to look and to listen. The women gesticulate, mumble and howl. A stir runs amongst them, lifting their hair, making their legs and arms light, dilating their pupils.

Skihack sets forth down the path; Blozzip behind him. The others crowd after.

Old Huckar hangs back. He bellows and roars at them. The company hesitates.

Skihack returns and comes up to him, followed by Blozzip. They cluck and gesticulate.

Blozzip raises his club.

One click is enough.

Old Huckar softens and sinks on his haunches.

The others start out, Blozzip taking the lead now.

Huckar scrambles up and goes after them, trailing his spear, slightly unsteady, shouting and howling.

Thus leadership passes. Thus leaders go under and new ones spring up.

They go down the trail like leaves in the wind, prancing, chattering, swirling, receding.

Something subsides at the caves. Something seems to grow dull.

They hear them coming down on Boulder Rock; hear the tumult and the shouting drawing near; rising like a stream's head in cloudburst, filling the air with noise and excitement.

They see them come out on the flat open space where the grasses grow, swinging along, shouting, howling, screaming like horses and neighing, roaring like bulls of the bison, lowing like cows, screeching out hideous laughter, clashing their spears together.

Old Huckar amongst them, ambling along at his full trot, waddling from side to side on his stout, squat, crooked legs, bent at the knees; trailing his spear, holding his javelin; silent, looking neither to right nor to left.

But Blozzip is up at the head of them.

It was then and thus that Starga saw them going by, just as Carnack was setting out for The Haunt and all the brimming life of spring was coursing through her veins, pulsing and throbbing.

As it was that night, perhaps, or one soon after, when the hunters had returned, that she left the cave on Boulder Rock.

CHAPTER XV

BLOZZIP TAKES TO A CLUB

CARNACK builds another hut that fall, and a better one, after his return from Volcano Basin. But it is not his final one, and he does not undertake to spend the winter in it. Indeed, only fire, when it comes, makes that possible.

We find him, when the snows set in, back on Boulder Rock in the midst of Knumf's wives and babies. Does he miss Starga now; miss something in her that was not quite in the rest?

He misses her skill in tanning. He works out, in the cave, this winter, some sort of shoe. He tells us this very carefully in two sketches. But he has to prepare the leather himself to get it sufficiently soft. That is one of the sketches.

The shoes are awkward enough; two rolls of leather at right angles, fastened together with thongs laced through holes, with a piece of skin wrapped over the heel where the two rolls meet and the end of one roll closed for the toes. No doubt they leaked atrociously, and they must have been constantly coming off. Nevertheless they were some protection for bare feet against the snow and ice.

Although Starga, who made Carnack's leather soft, dresses Blozzip's skins now, he has no shoes like them.

Sooash, we notice, youngest and fairest and the favorite of Huckar's four wives, and daughter to Palupe, joins the cave this winter, unmistakably as an addition to Knumf's domestic group; an innovation in cave life which that engaging and sophisticated traveller may have introduced from the people amongst whom he had been living, or which Sooash, unable to resist his charms, may have improvised. Perhaps economic considerations also weighed with sentiment in her defection. Old Huckar is not the man that he was. It tells in his hunting. But Sooash has become accustomed to the luxuries of life with which he has supplied her, and Knumf, with Carnack's flints at his disposal, contrives well to supply them. Huckar does nothing about it, apparently. Perhaps he is glad to be relieved of her demands. Perhaps he still reels from Blozzip's blow. The other three stay by. They are too far blown to be infected with Sooash's conduct.

The winter slips away without event beyond these spoken of. At one time the men from Shoulder Hill come for Carnack, apparently, or Knumf, or both, to go with them on a bison drive in the basin. Possibly they have designs upon a bear. It is before Sooash puts in her appearance at the cave; their visit could have nothing to do with that. Skihack is again spokesman.

Carnack, I have no doubt, sees Loof from time to time. I can believe that they have a rendezvous now and then down amongst the slender pines in front of the cave, or at the head of the lake, Loof slipping in close to the settlement and calling Carnack, or Carnack calling.

I can see Carnack striking out on a pleasant sunny morning across the virgin snow, sparkling smooth and white on the valley floor, with the pine-mottled ridges afloat in an eerie light beyond, to hunt the little animals whose tracks straggle here and there.

The sunlight gleams and flashes. The man looks this way and that. The water of the brook runs black through open places in the ice; swift, silent, arching over hidden rocks. Carnack leaps across; stands in the snow; utters the wolf-call; the long ululation; pushes through, perhaps, to The

Haunt, putting his new shoes to the test in the drifts and on the icy hillsides where the snow thaws by day and freezes when the sun is gone. Now and then he stops and calls, and waits.

As he goes, at the foot of the ridge, on a rock, from the covert of a bush, Loof appears; notched ear cocked; eager; waving his tail; howling softly; trying to say something. Or he may be far off in the mountains on a distant hunt, and does not come at all.

And at night, when the moon is white and cold over the snowfields, and the black pines stand out, and all the people in the caves huddle close, stirring in the cold, I can hear the lonely howl lift and swell and float and die away. The others lie stark with dread. But Carnack. . . . Out there . . . Loof . . . Chin lifted . . . Ears back . . . Eyes closed to slits, glinting in the moonlight . . . On his haunches . . . Tail in the snow . . .

Thus the winter runs away, before the rampart of rock Carnack has thrown up across the cave against it, and underneath the shoes he had sewn together to tread it down with, and spring comes forth at last. The snow breaks up into patches on the hills, the waters come out in the valley, a faint flush of green pushes up through the grass of other

years, the buds begin to wax and shine, rains wash
the sky of the last vestige of its grey wintry veil,
leaving it tender and pale, blinking its eyes and
reviving; and Carnack sets out.

That spring Blozzip takes to carrying a club.

We have seen him with one before on occasion.
But not always has he had one with him. Henceforth, however, he is never seen without one.

Possibly he snatches it up as a delayed reply to
Carnack's bow and arrow, or to a threat he feels
but cannot understand or cope with in him.

Possibly it is an answer, the only one he can
think of, to a strange confusion over Starga. He
may be finding something lacking in her, or something that bewilders him about her, so he seizes a
club that he can understand.

Or perhaps he simply comes to prefer it above
the javelin as a hunting weapon. He is to prove
himself capable with it, throwing it farther and
faster and straighter than his javelin.

Or he may have laid his hand by chance on one
that so suits his fancy by its size and weight and
balance and proportions that he keeps it by him for
sheer joy in its perfection.

The club that Blozzip hits upon gives us an idea
of his prodigious strength. It is as thick as a

man's arm with a knob on the end of it as big as two fists. Evidently it is the stem of a tree with the root gnarl left on. When he carries it, it dangles to the ground. Yet we see him flourishing it about and hurling it great distances. He could break a leg or a back with it at fifty yards, if we trust to the scale of drawings in which we see him using it. No doubt he could do for a bear with it quite handily, crushing in its skull with one blow. Luckily it was not the one he employed on Huckar's head.

We will speak of the first use we see him make of it.

Wolves, we are both told and know, were an evil to the people of the caves.

They not only laid a heavy toll on the food supply and kept food animals scattered and wary when they did not kill them, but they also committed depredations on the citizens themselves.

Hunting in packs, swift, strong, cunning and fierce, they often picked up straying children or even attacked groups of them. When hard pressed by hunger they no doubt did not hesitate to rush a solitary hunter. We have seen the fate of Starga's father.

So there was enmity against them amongst the

men of Shoulder Hill. When they found one they slew it on sight, if they could, and when they knew of a pack they got together and hunted them.

Thus we find Blozzip, on a day long enough after the coming of spring for the wolves to have whelped that year, coming upon a den of them under a rock and slaying all the pups, with his club, first accounting for the mother, who is seen lying dead on top of the rock with her head smashed in.

But the father, a huge, fearsome beast, eludes him. We see him standing at a distance, gnashing his fangs.

In due time we are told that wolves are running amuck in the village.

A fierce pack, led by a monstrous wolf, descends upon the caves when the men are away, terrifying the women, making off with a child or two. Carnack takes pains to show us the very incident; a dozen wolves or so, with the huge one at their head.

Huckar is at home that day, and casts a javelin at the leader of the pack, without effect. The gigantic fellow is too nimble for him; snarls, lays back his ears, and runs off.

There is a great commotion when the men come drifting back, by ones and twos and threes, toward the close of day, from the hills and the forests and plains; much shouting and getting together and waving of spears as they learn what has happened; hear the tale from the women; see the signs of it; mangled remains.

The gathering and the excitement grow with each returning hunter. Huckar comes down from his cave with club and spear, shouting, gesticulating, telling them what has occurred; how he defended the caves; how many wolves there were; assuming leadership again on the strength of it. Until Blozzip appears, striding forward, with Skihack, swinging his club, to see what has happened, throwing the deer he is bringing onto the ground.

Let us say, if you wish, that one of the children was Blozzip's.

He turns on Old Huckar ferociously, lifts up his club. Old Huckar avoids him; tells how many the wolves were; like the leaves on the oak tree, like the dust on the ground; points out where his javelin struck, shows how the leader evaded it.

And so the commotion continues till nightfall; the wailing of women, the crying of children, the shouting of men, the hollow beat of their feet on the ground as they trample and gesture.

On the morrow at daylight they set out, following the trail of the pack, picking out the huge pads of the leader in the welter of footmarks.

Carnack knows nothing about it. He is spending the night at The Haunt, where he spends all of them now.

Carnack, at daylight, comes out of his hut, giving the wolf-call; sending it skyward; rising and swelling and falling away; lifting again in full-throated ululation high above the incessant rustling of the waterfall, penetrating rocky glades, floating vibrantly to the tops of nearby ridges.

Carnack has seen little of his companion since he came to The Haunt this spring. Loof has affairs of his own, it would seem. Now and then he appears for a season, but leaves again hurriedly. Carnack calls him now and then. But no matter.

Carnack looks up and down; at the rocks, at the trees; at the sunlight creeping into the glade. He fills up his lungs. He goes to the spring-pool and scoops up a drink, shaking the drops off his chin, throwing back the water left in his palm. Two or three deer give way for him at the pool, coming back to finish drinking when he turns away. Others are browsing in the meadow. Birds are a-twitter again in the bushes and oak boughs. The breeze stirs and turns over, sighing and stretching. A squirrel scolds. A spider resumes spinning its web in the oak tree.

Carnack picks up a flint, turns it this way and that to see where he left off and where to begin, takes up his hammer-stone, and starts in: tick, tick, tick, clink; tick, tick, tick, ting; the pieces fly off, and the spear-head takes form. The sun climbs up and finds him there, squatting on his lean, lithe haunches.

He finishes the spear-head, lays it down, and looks around. The deer have departed. He reaches for the meat he brought with him on his last trip to Boulder Rock, shakes off the ants and the sand, bits of leaf and grass, tears off a shred with his teeth, chews and swallows, tears off another, takes a third, puts what is left on the ground, in the leaves and the grass, gets up, looks around, walks down to the brook and wades across.

The brook is making a sound like the sound of the young of the cave men in amongst the oaks in front of Shoulder Hill, heard from a distance in the cool of the day, or around the mouths of the caves when the men are away. The water that makes such a pleasant sound now where he is will soon be shouting down the waterfall. The water

goes, but the brook and the talk stay where they
are. Why does not the water stay still in one place
like the trees and the rocks? How can the sound
stay there when the water that makes it does not?
The rocks stay where they are, but make no noise.

He follows the rivulet down to the crag where
it leaps into the cañon, turns the shoulder of the
hill and makes his way to the bench where his pictoliths are, crawling along the face of the buttress
that flanks the valley's mouth with strong toes and
nimble knees.

Far off in the hills he hears shouts of the hunters.

He looks around for a hammerstone, picks up
a graving tool, a long splinter of flint that he has
worked down to a fine, sound point, and falls to
work where he left off the last time; click, click,
scritch, scratch, click, click, with his graving tool
against the surface and his hammer-stone delicately
tapping.

The hunters are still in the hills.

The sun gets too hot for him. He flings down
his implements and returns to the nook in The
Haunt, squatting in the shade with his back to the
rock.

The hunters are near in the hills. He can hear
them, voice for voice, shout for shout, in full career

after something up on the ridge. Is it a bear, he wonders?

He picks up the piece of meat left from breakfast and finishes it.

The sound of the hunters is coming his way.

They will not come there; they do not do that.

The bushes in the gulch above him stir and rattle.

He sees the shaggy tawniness of a wolf.

It is Loof.

Panting heavily. Tongue hanging out. His sides heave. There is a droop about the eyes.

He glances at Carnack, staggers up to the spring, laps it eagerly, stopping to swallow.

He goes over to Carnack, lays his muzzle on his knee, presses it there for a moment; then steals hurriedly into the hut.

The hunters are coming.

Carnack leaps to his feet; quickly squats down again.

He pulls his coup-de-poing close to him. He has lashed it to a handle by this time. It has become an axe in his hands.

He gathers his arrows and lays them beside him. He sets his bow handy.

He hears Blozzip's boom; Skihack's skreel.

He hears them coming down the gulch toward the spring.

The bushes crash.

He can see their tops swaying.

They part.

Blozzip leaps down by the springside.

Skihack comes after; Palupe, and Heetow; Skook and Old Huckar.

Carnack springs to his feet, coup-de-poing in his hand.

Blozzip stands facing him, bear skin garments awry, thighs scratched and bleeding, his hair mixed with leaves and sticks, his chest matted into curls and hooks of strong hair by sweat, enormous lips parted, teeth gleaming between them, the light of the chase-lust aflame in his eyes, his great club in his hand. Coarse, grizzled hair and shreds of red flesh adhere to the end of it. Stains smear it. He towers there clutching it, bristling, with Palupe and Heetow behind him; Skihack and Skook.

What the talk is we must guess.

Has a wolf been that way?

A denial.

Tracks seen by the spring-side. A sniff at the hut.

Blozzip swings his club down on it, crushes it in,

CARNACK LEAPS UPON BLOZZIP. BLOZZIP TOTTERS AND REELS. THE REST FALL ON CARNACK, TOOTH AND CLUB, CLAW AND SPEAR.

scatters the rushes and branches with three swings of his club.

Loof disappears in a twist and a flash of grey fur, snarling and snapping, into the bushes. Javelins follow him but he is too quick; too surprising.

Carnack leaps upon Blozzip, brings down his coup-de-poing; his new-fashioned club-axe.

Blozzip totters and reels.

The rest fall on Carnack, tooth and club, claw and spear.

A stir in the bushes. Loof rushes out. He slashes at Palupe, cuts deep into Skihack, turns upon Heetow, terrifies, scatters them, flashing from one to the other, avoiding their clubs and their spears, his hot breath on their throats.

Carnack and Blozzip have grappled; too close for club use.

It is here that our picture arrests them.

The rest we must guess. The details, that is. Carnack prevails; or rather their dread of him, long growing, no doubt, and brought to a climax by this league with a wolf, just discovered.

The next picture shows Blozzip accounted for, prone on the ground; and the others in flight, with the wolf-dog pursuing.

Carnack picks up his bow, but Skihack has broken the arrows.

There the scene leaves us.

What will the next step be?

The secret is out.

What will come after?

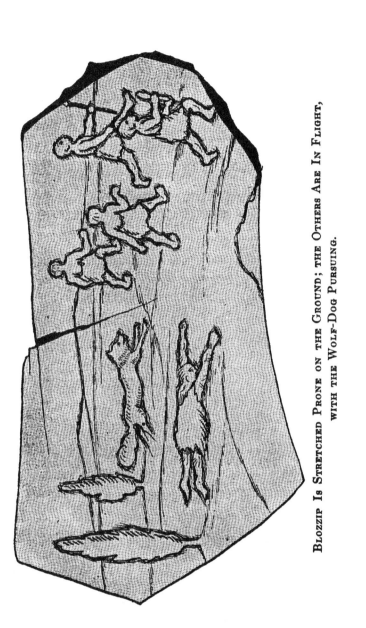

BLOZZIP IS STRETCHED PRONE ON THE GROUND; THE OTHERS ARE IN FLIGHT, WITH THE WOLF-DOG PURSUING.

Chapter XVI

The Bringer of Life

CARNACK first disposes of Blozzip, when the the others are gone; picks him up, slings him over his shoulder, carries him, limp and dangling, to the top of the trail by the waterfall, and dumps him down the rocky chute, flinging his hunting club, welted with gore, after him. The others, no doubt, come and get him, or he comes to himself and makes his way home alone.

He next mends his arrows. This takes a day or two; finding new shafts, whittling them down and fixing the points to them. They are unseasoned and heavy, but the best he can do.

Each dusk he gathers some berries and eats them, and some roots from the brookside, and cresses; shooting a rabbit for Loof in the cañon below, perhaps.

Loof does not leave him now. The wolf senses protection and the need to protect. A new bond is between them which never is broken. The last wilful wildness, the last depredation, succumbs to that day in the flat when they succored each other.

At night they lie together in the wreckage of the hut; Loof curled up beside the man, sleeping alertly, on sense against danger; Carnack watching the stars glisten overhead through the oaks, listening, as he falls asleep, to the rustle of the leaves in the evening breeze, the soft purl of the brook, the plash of the waterfall, the rhythmic trills in the grass, all the secret noises of the night; thinking of the day and yesterday and tomorrow; of Blozzip and Huckar, Skihack and Heetow, Laa'aa and Blish, Inkin and Starga; wondering; wistful. Is it surprising if he fills his pictures and his life henceforth with this wolf-dog; reflects toward him a responsive, devoted, unexacting love—for the first time, perhaps, on earth, that love has been expressed by man toward any other creature, man or beast?

On a morning soon after the affray in The Haunt we see Carnack catching a fish with his hands in a pool in the cañon below, and eating it.

He has made up his mind what to do. They had wanted to kill Loof, and he would not let them. They had wanted to kill him, but Loof would not let them. Now they would want to kill them both.

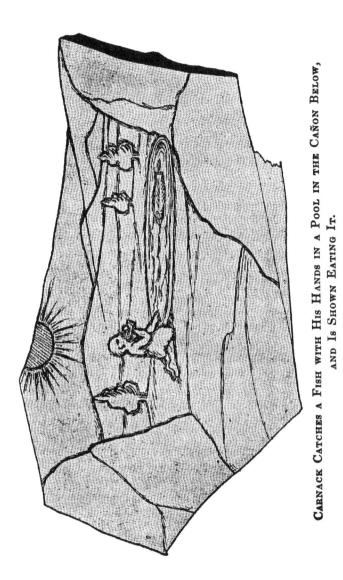

CARNACK CATCHES A FISH WITH HIS HANDS IN A POOL IN THE CAÑON BELOW, AND IS SHOWN EATING IT.

He has decided what to do. His plans are made.

Loof is with him, and his bow and many arrows.

They start on the trail up the cañon that leads over many ridges to the lake.

Loof, trotting at Carnack's heels, lifts his nose and pricks an ear to learn what lies ahead.

Carnack stops to shoot a squirrel, which they share. He is expert now at hitting the mark, although his arrows are still without feathers.

He marches steadily forward with strong thrusts of his legs. Loof sniffs and looks up at him. The wolf's tail swings from side to side as he trots behind.

They reach the lake, round the head of it and come to the fork in the trail; one leading to the cluster of pines and Boulder Rock, the other to the caves at Shoulder Hill.

Carnack turns at once to the right, into the one that leads to the caves; to the settlement; to the men of Shoulder Hill.

Loof follows.

Down by the river and up past the thickets straight forward they go, and so into the oaks in front of the caves.

The men are gathering for a day's hunting. Some of them have left.

They see Carnack and the wolf.

Carnack stands with his bow in his hand, Loof at his knee.

Hush falls over the hill and the caves and the oaks. The men weave about, muttering, watching the man and the wolf.

Carnack takes a step forward.

Blozzip is there. And Old Huckar. The men gather together. The women and children peep out of their caves. Starga is watching, from Blozzip's.

Carnack moves steadily forward, with an arrow poised on his bow-string. Others are tucked in a fold of his garment.

Loof keeps pace with him, head down, tail drooping, rolling an eye up at Carnack.

Blozzip steps forward, followed by Huckar. Skihack moves at his elbow. Two or three others fall in behind them.

Carnack keeps on within bow-shot; within the range of a javelin or Blozzip's mighty club, if he should throw it.

Carnack stops, sweeps out an arm toward them, pointing to Loof and to them and himself; shouting out syllables; trying to tell them. He walks

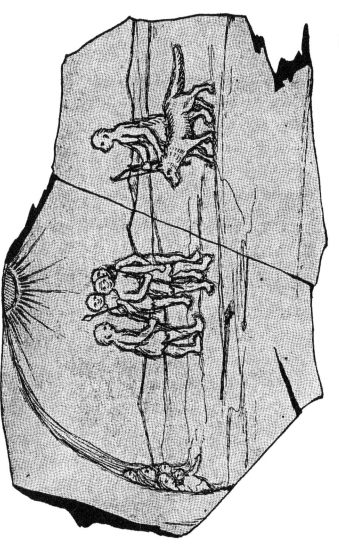

The Men (Shown in This Pictolith) Weave About, Watching the Man and the Wolf.
Women and Children Peep Out of the Caves.

up and down, making gestures, with Loof at his side; lays his hand on the head of the animal.

This is the scene we have, cut into the rock.

Not long afterward—it might be that very day, for it is the adjacent picture—we see the two on top of Boulder Rock. Loof seems ill at ease, but trustful and submissive. Knumf's wives huddle together in panic, their babes in their arms. Knumf picks up his bow, but Carnack, of course, forbids him to use it. Inkin comes up. Moox, fat and slow, arouses herself to drive off the wolf. Carnack prevents her, but Loof keeps his distance.

There is another picture—a tiny one—which I choose to believe belongs to this time, for all that it is tucked away in a vacant triangle of a much later period, in which Carnack seems to be trying to tell us of an attempt he is making to establish understanding between Starga and Loof. Loof appears willing enough, but Starga, although not precisely reluctant, is timid and doubtful.

It is of the highest importance to know what this signifies, but the best we can do is to guess. Everything goes to show that the picture is one of those interpolated afterthoughts which prove so confusing, and so illuminating when deciphered, but nothing about the picture fixes its exact time and place in the sequence of events, which now become more crowded and vital.

Has Starga stolen down by another way from Shoulder Hill to meet him in the thickets? The scene apparently is in the thickets by the trail. Has she seen through to something for the first time? Is a new light breaking in on her concerning this man? Is she beginning now to turn to it?

Does Carnack write the picture down long afterward because many things must first transpire before he can know what it means—her coming to him there, after she has seen him with Loof, facing the men?

Or is it just a chance meeting down in the thickets at any time as he comes and goes about his business after the people in the caves are more used to him and his wolf? Starga out for berries or nuts; Carnack bringing flints?

Does he put it where it is, some summer afternoon, in idle reminiscence, filling up a little corner of the rock with a pleasant recollection?

He shows no other attempts at any time to bring about a friendship for Loof with any person in particular. Loof and Inkin get along, but that is their affair.

For a time these two have to take to the hunt in

earnest. Either the hunters at The Hill institute a boycott against Carnack because of his strange league with the enemy, or their dread of him keeps them away from him and him from them, for the flint business lags and we find Carnack and Loof, with bow and arrow, in far places out in the hills or down by the lake; quite another lake, I think, from the one we know—and even in Volcano Basin. Apparently it is not pleasant for them where the others hunt.

By degrees, however, the taboo, from what ever cause it springs, begins to wear off. The hunters do not like to go back to chipping flints. They prefer Carnack's better ones. They have no time to bother with their own. They make overtures. Perhaps Knumf intervenes, reviving a trade that brought profit to him. They cease to make threatening gestures when they pass at a distance. Business revives, and we see Carnack back in The Haunt once more, Loof by his side in the shade of the oak, chipping his flints and getting out spear-shafts.

Carnack has time now to rebuild his hut again, making a bigger and better one; one intended to withstand the winter and accommodate him and his dog. Instead of limp and crooked branches he uses straight, stiff poles in the side walls, with crotches left in them, apparently, to support the roof; lashing them together more or less, weaving branches in, and plastering all with mud. This time, also, his roof does not rest vaguely against the rock of the inner wall, but it is supported there by a rafter which he rigs up on crotched poles. Furthermore he builds a skeleton to carry the thatching of boughs and the weight of the mud that he plasters them with. Rushes and reeds do not play such a part in the structure; although he seems to use them in the final layer on his roof. The doorway is the same—a trifle larger, perhaps.

But the time is not yet. Whatever his intentions when he builds so well, he is to have one more winter in the cave. He stays in his hut until the snow flies and after. But he gives it up. It is too cold. Even with Loof for a nest-fellow.

Chapter XVII

Fire Comes

CARNACK has little to say about the winter. No doubt the expansive and expanding presence of Knumf with his three wives and their joint progeny, with Moox, who has aroused herself to perpetual warfare with Loof, forever shrilling after him, makes The Haunt seem undesirable. But there is nothing for it. He stays and fights the battle for himself and for his dog.

Once we see him—in his shoes—at The Caves. Loof is with him; rather uncomfortable, perhaps, but unmolested. What his errand is, is not made clear. He has a skin in his hand. Is he collecting a debt or having Starga tan it for him, making it soft, as she knows how to do? That would be an interesting development; but we have little warrant for assuming it. Starga is not in the picture.

He hunts a good deal, possibly to get away from the cave; to have something else to do. Once, apparently, he gets up to The Haunt; unless he is indulging in a bit of imaginative composition when he shows the place in wintertime—a delightful little picture, with the snow sifting down and piled up on the bushes. Neither he nor the wolf are in evidence, and there is nothing to indicate what the drawing is intended to convey; no event, present, precedent, or consequent. Excepting that the hut has not fallen down. He and Loof may be inside it. They may be spending some time there.

Old Huckar has fallen still further. He no longer inhabits the largest cave. Blozzip has taken it; and Skihack—there is some doubt about this, but I am quite sure of it—has moved into Blozzip's old one. Huckar contents himself with a den at the edge of the cluster, where we see him for a year or two with his three remaining wives, going hunting with the hunters still, sitting on the edge of the pow-wows they presently commence to hold—a contrivance of Skihack's—doddering about, hanging on to the fringe, huge and heavy, stunned and bemused, not so much from the blows he has suffered as from the fact that they were struck, until, after one last grand affair of buffets and brawn, he disappears into an unknown fate and his three wives fade away, all of the sons and daughters having long since been absorbed and lost into the crowd that swarms the caves.

In the spring Carnack and Loof accompany the men from Shoulder Hill on the first big hunt in the Basin. We see them setting out. Loof is no doubt a great help to them, turning horses for them, heading off bison, cutting colts and calves out of the herd, bringing down one now and then. They can understand that. His fleetness gives them an advantage they have never had before. Carnack has his bow and arrows with him. No doubt they are beginning to understand them, too.

When they return from this hunt Carnack and Loof move back to The Haunt. Loof, I imagine, is pretty well pulled this way and that in the season of mating. Perhaps he decamps for a while. Some one suggests, on the strength of a cutting which shows him sitting upon a rock, baying and calling, that he brings his mate to the little vale; but the evidence is slight. Carnack would have pictured the family in that case.

He has a long session at the pictoliths that spring. He has a great deal to report by this time. The last he had set down—this largely is guesswork, but not too far astray, we know—was on the day of the episode in The Haunt, when Loof and he fought off the cave men. There has been much since that time to put down. He is busy till summer, with this and his flinting.

Then fire comes.

There are some who deny it, but the record is clear.

The season is dry, to begin with. The threads in the sign of the waterfall, the sign of The Haunt, have dwindled to two.

Carnack is now getting out handles for spears and for javelins as well as his arrow-shafts. Knumf seems to have drummed up quite a trade in these, and Carnack makes good ones.

He cuts them with his coup-de-poing from thickets nearby that he knows of, lops off the limbs, and brings them in to The Haunt, where he works by the spring side.

The first thing to do is to strip off the bark. This he does. Then he whittles them round.

This done, he scrapes them down with an excellent flint, smooth-edged and sharp. Fischer found such a scraper, unbelievably perfect, and has it in Hamburg.

When he has finished, the shaft for the spear or the javelin, or for his own arrows, is shiny and sleek, even and flawless.

And down by his feet is a pile of fine shavings and wood dust.

The summer goes on, the pile keeps increasing. It scatters about, and gets dryer and dryer.

On a day, late on a hot afternoon, Carnack has flints to make. Spearheads for Blozzip, or one for Old Huckar.

Carnack gathers his hammer-stones where he can find them. Their shape and their hardness is vital. Also, their weight. They need to be heavy, but handy; have striking power without being clumsy.

Amongst them are favorites. This one is best for the first heavy fracture of flakes from the nodule, that one for more delicate tapping, another to finish the rough work and prepare for the process of pressing the last tiny flakes off. He brings them from distances, picked up at random, ready made to his hand, heavy and balanced; under cliffs, out of stream beds, in cañons where water has tumbled and worn them.

Some of the best are yellow or reddish, and exceedingly heavy; fragments of pyrite, laden with iron.

There is one in particular. He finds it one day, let us say, just over the ridge in Three-Quarters

Cañon, high up in the watercourse, under a cliff. The cliff is still there, and such fragments.

Ages have already rolled this stone about and gnawed it with wind and with rain and with torrent. It is smooth, with perfect shape and balance; a shaft for the hand with a knob poised on top of it; small enough for great precision of blow, but heavy enough to knock off the first flakes—the use that he puts it to, tumbling it down on the nodule with a deft turn of the wrist, arresting its fall at the moment of contact, giving a tap instead of a follow-through blow.

I can see him returning with it just before nightfall along the cheek of Picture Cañon—what his name was for the cañon where we found the pictoliths, if he had one for it, is, of course beyond a guess—along the very path, perhaps, that led us to the pictoliths two hundred and fifty centuries later at sunfall.

He has come that way, which is the long way home, to have a look at the pictoliths; study the one he is working on; plan the next one. He stops in front of them, on the broad bench that the ages have since sheered away. He puts in a line to finish a figure; promises himself to go farther tomorrow, or the day after that. But first he has flints to get out.

He lingers to watch the red sunlight sloping over the tops of the ridges. The summer has been long and dry, the grass has dried out, the animals are lean and scarce and wary. The air crackles with heat. There is no sign of rain. The sky is flat and hard—flat and hard and yellow and red, like a leaf on the ground. The crystal shout of the brook in the cañon beneath him is not half what it was. The laughing waterfall has grown sad and silent.

The day is fast sinking out of the hills. Shadows pour into the cañons. The evening hush is in the air.

He skirts the rocky escarpment, enters The Haunt and proceeds to The Nook, throwing down his bow and his arrows, and examines his hammerstone; his treasure; his prize; eager to use it; eager to try and to prove it; hefting it; swinging it.

Too late to begin now. He scarcely could see to strike. True the sparks make a light, but not before striking, and they go out at once.

Now he is sitting, on a hot afternoon, not many days afterward, in the midst of the shavings from spear-shanks and arrow shafts, working out flints.

He has his new hammerstone.

He rolls over the nodules, one after the other; selects one; tosses and turns it; determines its angles; grasps it; poises it; raises his hammer-stone. Click! Click! Click! Sitting there alone, in the midst of the shavings and scrapings like tinder; fine as dust, much of it, and fully as dry. Up in The Nook, by the spring and the tree; with Loof curled beside him, chin on paws, lazily blink-ing, lifting an eyelid, rolling an eye, settling his tongue in his teeth for a nap, breathing deep, fetch-ing a sigh, dozing off, flicking an ear, cocking it in his sleep at some sound in the bushes.

Sparks fly at each tap. Carnack is used now to that. It is something they always do, with this stone and some others. At first they frightened him; some of these stronger sparks.

Before long he smells something; unlike any ani-mal, bird, bush, or broken stone.

He looks up, looks around, sniffing the air.

He sees something moving; curling up from the shavings; slender and coiling; twisting and turn-ing; a thing like a snake, but it is not one.

It separates, vanishes, comes up again.

He can see the ground through it.

Then the breeze takes it. It grows bigger and bigger.

It has a red head. It is eating the shavings; clinging on; sinking in.

This is the thing that he smelled. Where else has he smelled it?

Then he remembers; sees what it is; leaps upward, terrified, shrieking, scattering flints, flakes and hammerstones with the spring of his powerful legs; as others, no doubt, had done on similar occasions, sprinkled back along the cold, dark centuries that lay behind Shoulder Hill and Seafar Basin.

Loof bounds to his feet, stiff and bristling, fangs showing, dancing off sidewise, seeking the danger.

Carnack flees to the brook; makes a stand; turns and looks back.

The thing is still waving, growing larger and larger. He can see from the brook.

He comes back, slowly, with caution. This is what the others had not done.

Loof steals at his heels.

Thus fire.

Thus Carnack.

Thus the great discovery. Up there in the mountains. On that hot afternoon in the summer, twenty-five milleniums ago.

He stands still and stares.

The thing that was not a snake has become like a tree, branching and waving. The top of it flutters, like leaves. The roots heap and heave, creeping into the shavings. Little red vines climb up in the tree. They look like a wolf's tongue. Like Loof's. Except redder. And yellow.

A puff of wind bounces down out of the gulch, twisting and twirling the tree, sucking up tongues from the roots. More tongues leap out of the center; the root knot.

He grows frightened again. The thing gets too big. He picks up his bow and an arrow to kill it.

He shoots it; flings a shaft into it; quivering, vibrant, stuck in the root bed.

Tongues, red and yellow, begin to run over the shaft of the arrow.

He reaches to pluck it out.

A tongue stings him.

He lets go of it quickly.

It falls back in the red roots and the tongues and disappears slowly, with many tongues licking it. Nothing is left of it.

He remembers the arrow he shot into Grash-po-Nash.

Something comes over him, exciting, terrifying. But he is not afraid now.

He picks up a shaft of another one, spoiled in the making, and throws it into the tree that is not a tree, the tongues that are not tongues.

The tongues that are not tongues fall hastily on it.

The tree that is not a tree goes soaring apace.

He feels something warm from it; a warmth like the sun's.

Sees the light of the sun kindle on Loof in the gathering dusk.

He had not seen the sun go.

Something stupendous swells in his heart, struggles for form in his thoughts; shadowy visions of sun in the winter, light in the darkness. Too shadowy yet. Not even a faint premonition. But something that stirs him.

The will of God in him.

Meanwhile Loof looks on, curious, indulgent.

He throws in more arrows. Good ones. The tongues rush together and leap.

He can see the smell floating about in the air.

He goes over to Loof.

He squats down to watch it; this offspring of Grash-po-Nash; this son of the sun.

He is not afraid.

The others feared Loof, but Loof is his friend.

The others fear Grash-po-Nash; but this is his friend.

The thing leaps and flutters, but stays where it is. It does not go after the arrow-shafts lying close by.

Grash-po-Nash lives in a rock, and cannot get out of it. This thing lived in a rock, but he got it out. Out of two of them; this one and that one.

He throws in a long piece of sapling, cured and dry, ready for shaving.

The tongues lick it in two.

He throws in the two ends.

They vanish, slowly, covered with tongues.

He throws in an old hammerstone; some pieces of flint.

The tongues coil around them; curl away.

He throws in a piece of a horse that has been lying around. The tongues lap thirstily at it. The flesh shrivels up as if alive, sputters and hisses. The smell of it comes to his nostrils.

He is quieter now. He throws on more sticks; pieces left over. They burn. The horse-meat lies deep in their midst, growing smaller, oozing juices that trickle and hiss.

His wood is all gone, save his arrows and spear. The thing flutters down, dies away, gasps, turns to a red glow. Just as Grash-po-Nash does, after one of its struggles to free itself.

Most of the light goes away, and much of the warmth. Darkness has come unawares. He looks out in surprise, into its depths, where the rocks and the trees were like day in the dance of the tongues.

He picks up one of the rocks he threw in, but, although he can see nothing on it, it bites him.

He pokes in with an arrow. The flints are untouched. That much he can see by the light of the embers.

He forks out the horse-flesh and smells it. He ventures his teeth in it, looks up with surprise, and consumes it voraciously, leaving nothing, for once, for his dog.

He wishes for more of it. Wishes for more of the sun heat. Wishes the light was not gone.

But he knows how to get them again! Knows how to coax them out of the rocks into the dust heaps. Out of the heavy red hammerstone and the nodule of flint!

He turns in for the night; crawls into his hut. Loof follows.

He pauses to look where the thing was and to look at the stars.

Tomorrow he will kindle another.

Chapter XVIII

Skies of Brass

THUS came fire to the use of man, on the lonely hills of Utah, twenty thousand years before the burning bush on the flanks of Sinai was beheld by another dreamer and seer for his people.

How long it is before Carnack learns how to coax the fire out of the rocks without fail when he wishes to, how long it takes him to note that he need not wait for the parings from his arrow-shafts to accumulate but that any fine dust and scrapings from wood or twigs will do; how soon he finds out that if he feeds it sticks fallen from trees or broken off from those that are bare or fallen down it will live but that if he gives it soft branches from trees that have leaves on it will not, while if he offers it water to drink it dies quickly, with a great hissing commotion, we can only guess.

How he learns how to nurse it by blowing it and to keep it by keeping it covered, how he finds out how to cook—that the horse meat and deer meat and rabbits need not be thrown into the fire, but taste just as good on a stick held above it or covered with stones that have been in the fire—how he discovers the need and the method of sheltering it, building a screen for it in front of the door of his hut so the heat can come in—and the smoke, we can guess—, how to protect it from snow and the rain, are questions that any can answer who wish to. It is not down on the rocks.

The scientists, naturally, say he did not. That he could not have done so in so short a time. They say he borrowed and imitated. They say that Knumf brought fire. That the cave people always had had it. They account for it every way; but they leave out revelation. Deny it to Carnack. Deny it to us.

Whereas what but revelation, what but inspiration, what but the will of God working in us both to will and to do, has been the source of any good and permanent step in human progress and unfoldment? "Every good gift and every perfect gift is from above, and cometh down from the Father of lights." By whom and to whom do they come down if not by and to the sons of God, made in His image and likeness? Was not Carnack, who took fire and blessed with it, a son of God? Just as we are?

"With whom is no variableness, neither shadow of turning," James concludes.

Carnack does not run off to Shoulder Hill with fire, as he had done with his bow, and with Loof eventually.

He has learned better than that. Instead he keeps it to himself, even being careful to conceal it from the others, I imagine.

He does not, for instance, build one on Boulder Rock.

Boulder Rock is rather empty again. The sociable Knumf, growing lonely where he is, betakes himself, before the first snow flies, up to Shoulder Hill, where he ensconces himself alongside of Skihack in Blozzip's recent cave, celebrating the move by adding one more to his family group in the person of one of Huckar's daughters, if I am not mistaken. At the same time the second wife—the one between Sooash and the foreign woman,— passes from the scene, so he still has only three.

This move leaves Inkin alone with Laa'aa and Moox. It is possible that Inkin and Laa'aa mate, although there are strong reasons, later, to think that they did not. Moox is no good any more, and does not pretend to be. Carnack pays visits; gets meat; leaves his flints for Inkin to peddle. But he hunts more; saves himself the long walk down. Goes up in Three-Quarters Cañon, the edge of Volcano, far from The Haunt. With his bow and his dog. Inkin hunts also, by himself, and with the hunters. The flint trade grows leaner. Carnack makes barely enough for the hunters. He needs much less meat now for himself and the family, with Inkin providing, too.

Carnack spends the winter in The Haunt, in his hut, by his fire. We see him there, in the snow, and when the trees are bare; the smoke curling up; Loof lying beside him. They live on small animals, caught at a distance. Perhaps, now and then, he kills in The Haunt. It would hardly be necessary. They do not need much.

Feathers appear on his arrows that autumn. Where he got the idea is one of the mysteries that vexes the experts. Perhaps the suggestion came from sticks falling with leaves on their ends. That may have led to experiments; leaving leaves on an arrow shaft. Then feathers. Tied on with the dried gut of a squirrel. Or a fine thread of deer skin. Whatever the source, we find feathers in evidence; a notable step for the better in the speed and the range and the aim of his arrows.

His clothing improves, too. We have spoken of

his garments growing softer. Now he is sewing them—shaping them, almost. The sewing consists merely in lacing the edges together with buck-skin. The weather gets through, but the garments stay on and keep him more covered. He has capes down his arms. Closed sleeves never appear. The skirts are much longer, and closer; not flapping and flying. He tans these garments himself; he shows himself doing it.

The winter is a light one, with thin, dry snows and few rains. The sign of The Haunt—the waterfall symbol—still shows only two lines after the fall rains—if there are any.

Spring comes in early, pale and wan, sparse and yellow.

Not even now do the threads in the symbol, the signs of the stages of water, grow into three.

No freshets from the upper melting snows boom and cleanse the streams.

No boggy places form and spread in lowlands, promising grass throughout the season.

The faint flush of green that runs over the plains and the valleys and up on the hillsides, withers, and dies away.

The leaves on the trees, unfolding tardily, stay

little and thin, grey, scattered along the branches, drooping and listless.

Every sun comes up brazen and goes down in copper.

The air is electrical, crackly and prickly, drying the skin, making the lips split.

The sky is naked and stretched, day after day. Nowhere a cloud. Nowhere a sign of one.

At night the hot wind moves. The stars leap and quiver; burning and flashing.

The lake in the valley shrinks into a huge, stale pool, dribbling a sick stream into the channel that carries down through The Gorge and into the Basin.

Seafar becomes a scorched, quivering plain.

The stunted grass lies parched and withered.

The leaves fall off in mid-season, yellow and juiceless.

Creeks dry down to sluggish oozes.

The spring in The Nook ceases to bubble.

The ribbon of water curling languidly over the dry lip of the little valley's mouth dwindles to a single brittle line.

Day after day, under the screenless sun, the hunters go and return.

Gaunt-cheeked women watch them, going and

coming. Children with hollow eyes stare at them. Game, at first, was still to be found on the highest ridges or about a few stagnant waterholes in Seafar Basin.

But little by little it vanishes off of the face of the earth.

No journey can be pushed far enough to emerge beyond the edge of the relentless pall from beneath which the wild beasts have fled.

The people are caught in a trap.

They fall back on roots and leaves for sustenance.

They crack old bones, and crunch them up in their ponderous jaws.

It is in the midst of this that Starga comes to Carnack in The Haunt.

What is her errand? What brings her?

Does she turn to him with a sense that he can help them; this man who makes sticks fly, tames animals, lives by himself and writes on the rock?

This man who is stronger than Blozzip, though not in his arms?

This man who is wiser than Skihack, though not against others?

This man who can make his own cave and live in it?

This man that others are fearful of?

What is it brings her? What does she hope for?
Carnack gives us the picture.

He has, on a day, shot an antelope; a little and
lean one. A sick one, perhaps, that could not get
away.

He chooses to cook it.

He comes back from the hunt to build up a fire.

First he lays out a handful of tinder—no lack of
it now!—then hunts up his flint and his hammer-
stone.

He clicks them together. The sparks do not
come at first, but he continues.

At last a few fly off into the tinder; but even in
this weather they do not ignite it at once.

Loof sits by, looking on. He is hungry. He
sniffs at the antelope.

Carnack keeps on, click, click, click, with his flint
down close to the tinder.

At last a spark catches. A tiny red glow bur-
rows in and brightens.

Carnack bends over it, nurses it, blows on it,
until it takes heart, glows higher and broadens, running deep into the dry, dusty shavings, bursting at
last into a tiny flame that creeps here and there,
igniting thicker parings, until he flings in some
twigs and a stick for it to fatten on.

When he looks up he sees Starga standing there, down by the brook, timid and frightened.

She has come up unawares; even Loof was off guard, intent on the antelope.

What is her errand?

She plainly is frightened; probably terrified at sight of fire.

What else could she be? Grash-po-Nash she and the others know about, throwing his flare on the sky at night, pulsing and coming and going, like the breath of a hunter following deer up a hill or horses across the plain, muttering and gurgling far away in the next basin, with now and then a shuddering, growling rumble through the earth and a mighty upheaval of stars and flame and smokedust beyond the intervening peaks. And the sun she knows; for is not Grash-po-Nash a piece of it that had fallen near them and still struggled to get back again?

Perhaps, now and then, in a storm, she has seen a spear from the sky pierce and devour a tree with the light and heat of the sun and of Grash-po-Nash. Possibly, too, she may have witnessed a forest fire, a spontaneous outburst in the midst of hot, dry weather like the present, catching and running from pine-ridge to pine-ridge, filling the air with crackle and smoke, lighting the night up like Grash-po-Nash. Carnack shows us a picture which can be nothing else.

All this is sufficiently terrifying.

But of intimate fire, familiar, close at hand, fed with sticks, bringing summer in winter and holding day fast in its fingers throughout the night; friendly; in one place; kept or put out at will; revived and called back; obedient servant; jolly companion; singing the song of its pine leaves; chattering; crackling; snapping its fingers; laughing and dancing; wrapping them warm in its blanket of fur-heat, she and her people know nothing.

To see Carnack making it, luring it out of the sticks and the stones, building it up, making it grow, ...

Whatever her errand, she does not complete it. She turns and flees instead. Carnack shows her hurrying off, down by the waterfall. Back to the others.

He must have understood, later, when he put down this picture, what her running away meant; understood its connection with events that developed at once.

He understood it when he drew her, in the next

picture, talking to Skihack and Blozzip in the oaks in front of the caves.

What followed is not surprising. What is surprising is that they were satisfied with what they did, and did not turn upon Carnack then and there and destroy him.

What interval passes between this conversation and the events which he next reveals there is no way of knowing. The series of pictures is immediately adjacent. They all are distinctly historical; written down afterward in the light of subsequent knowledge. For Carnack was absent himself. He got it from hearsay. From Starga, undoubtedly. Much later.

Conditions in the community have become more desperate than ever. Now and then some hunter brings in a lean, leathery animal which they all share. It melts like a snowflake. Blows fall over it; the strongest get most.

But most of the men have ceased hunting. They sit behind rocks in the shade of the oaks, while the women squat listless in the entrances to the caves, with their heads leaning on the walls. Emaciated children walk up and down.

Old Huckar's eye has grown dim. His shambling, ambling gate that has left so many men beside the way in his day has become an imbecile shuffle. He sits staring at the empty, sunparched hills and the grey, hot forests on the ridges, remembering other days. Now and then he mumbles and stiffens, with a flare in his eyes, recalling encounters, re-slaying bears juicy with meat; slaughtering bison.

Blozzip knocks his women about, baleful and sullen; including Starga. Skihack keeps out of his way. Knumf has become a tattered vagabond, stripped of his gay airs. Palupe sits silently, day after day, in front of his cave, not moving, letting the sun shine down, letting the shade come. Heetow goes off into the hills.

The sky is clanging, metallic, burnished and polished. Colors run through it at night and in mornings like heat upon copper; faint purples and yellows and greens and blues; iridescent, incandescent.

Eyes turn up to this brazen sky, eyes drawn and weary, morose and desperate, searching the mountain rims to the east, to the west, to the north and the south, for the huge white, undulent, towering, wooly clouds that come in the summer; spreading wide at their bases; climbing higher and higher into the blue, with the afternoon sun gleaming on them.

But ever the sky of shimmering brass, brittle and fleckless.

This is the state of affairs when Starga seeks Carnack, and comes back to tell what she found.

Skihack, I think, is the one who begins it.

It suited his genius to do it.

He stands up amongst them, turns his face to the south-west; turns it toward Grash-po-Nash.

Once before in a crisis like this in his lifetime the men had gathered together. He remembers it well in his youth. He went with them.

He mutters and mumbles, steps this way and that, turns about in his tracks, vents a shout now and then.

The others come trooping and singly—Blozzip, Palupe, Heetow, Skook, even Huckar and Knumf. They catch up his groaning and crooning. Some of them join in his steps.

An abhorrent, hideous, terrifying sound soon sets up in the midst of the woods; shouts, howls, screams, the thumping of feet. Skihack stands in the midst, weaving his body, leaping, gesticulating, waving his arms, pointing to the sky and Gash-po-Nash and to where the sun burns hot.

He makes signs to tell them of the fire that Carnack builds, sweeps his arm toward the sky, toward the caves where the women are, toward Grash-po-Nash. He twists and writhes; leaps and stamps; rolls his eyes, clicks his teeth, stretches and clenches his hands, howls and yells. Others join in a crescendo of frenzied excitement.

Up in the caves the onlooking women huddle and cower, gazing down amongst the oaks in fascinated terror. Many remember the last time. Others have heard, and been dreadful. Who will it be now? What blooming young maiden, ripe for mating?

At a turn in their dance, by sudden propulsion, without any signal, the howling, swarming group whirl off through the oaks down the wide path that leads through the thickets past the brook to the cave of Blish, or the trail to The Haunt.

Inkin is first to hear them approaching.

He is lying on the nest, weak and weary.

For a moment he believes it to be the rush of a storm; coming thunder; a torrent through boulders; a promise and presage of succor.

Then a gust of cold terror goes through him.

He does not remember, but knows what it means. No man could hear such a sound coming on through the woods, without understanding.

He runs out on the rock. Moox sits there sleeping, her head on the wall, making noises in her throat and flat nose. He runs back to the nest. Laa'aa is there. She looks up at him. He runs out on the rock again.

The noise has drawn nearer; a great, swelling roar, pierced by screeches and pulsed with the thudding of sticks on the ground.

He sees them down in the grass.

They enter the pines.

They come swarming up toward him.

He grasps up his bow.

Moox laughs.

He hears that; then a crash. Nothing more—but the sound of the screeching and stamping and howling going off up the trail toward the caves.

Or The Haunt.

He creeps back to the nest.

Someone has hurt him.

Laa'aa is gone.

CHAPTER XIX

GRASH-PO-NASH

THE pictoliths at this point are confusing.
We have the one of Laa'aa's seizure; the
men from the caves swarming up to Boulder Rock;
Inkin offering to stand them off single-handed with
his bow; Blozzip hurling the club which, we may
assume, fells him before he draws it.

We have one showing the sacrificial party approaching the volcano; marching through the night,
apparently, for the quarter moon is in the sky;
Laa'aa in the midst, with Skihack at her side.
Grash-po-Nash flames and flares in the distance,
sternly preparing for his bride. Not all of the men
are out. Only Skihack, Blozzip, Skook, Heetow
and two or three of the others. They have quieted
down and are dogged and sullen.

Carnack was not present at either of these scenes
or he would have said so. They are pure chroni-
cles, drawn from reports made by others and his
own general knowledge.

At the same time we have pictures of Carnack
and Loof—and a surprising third—marching off

across the plains of Volcano Basin under the same moon, apparently, that lights the way for Laa'aa; standing on the brink of the volcano, and coming back, the three of them, but otherwise alone.

Also there is one of Carnack at Boulder Rock, one at the caves, and one down by the lake where the trail crosses the inlet, in which Starga is with him.

The confusing thing about these pictures is that they are concentric to the key scene on The Rock, drawn apparently at random in a semi-circle around it with nothing in or out of them to suggest a beginning, end, or sequence.

What I gather from them is that Carnack is away when the men, half starved, terrified by the parched and yellow sky day after day, believing that the sun is angry with them because of Carnack's fire, which they have learned about, and worked upon by Skihack, go screaming and howling to get Laa'aa; that he finds out what has happened on his return, and sets out to rescue her.

He must have been at some distance from The Haunt and the trail leading through it and the gorge at the head of it into Volcano Basin and so to Grash-po-Nash, for he did not hear them pass. It is certain that they did not see him, in the mood they were in, or there might have been another story to tell—with no one to tell it.

He may have been off in Three-Quarters Cañon —which is unlikely, for that was too near the way they went—or he may have been up on the ridges at the head of the gulch that came down at The Nook. There is a deposit of flint up there, rather finer than that at the lake, although farther away, and he may have gone for a piece of it. Perhaps his graving tool was worn out and he wanted to get out another one from this finer, tougher, cleaner flint. But that is no matter. He was away, which was enough.

How and when did he learn of what had occurred? He may have noticed the tracks of the men when he returned to The Haunt; may have seen Laa'aa's footprints amongst the others, and divined the rest. He may have learned it when he went, later in the day, on some errand to Boulder Rock. He may have swung down from the ridge where the flint is by way of Shoulder Hill on his way home; a long route, but not an impossible one, if he had business there.

There is reason to believe that this is what he does. That he comes down the rocky bed of the stream behind The Hill and emerges on the flank of the caves after the departure of the party and when they are already well on their way to The Haunt, or through it. His appearance creates a commotion, he shows us in the drawing of him at the caves, which, we must suppose, depicts the scene. The men that are left are excited and threatening. No doubt it puzzles him. He does not stop to enquire, but swings wide through the oaks and heads for Boulder Rock, leaving his errand at the caves for another time and better tempers.

At the rock he finds Inkin lying in the nest, battered and swollen. Moox sits babbling in the sun. As well as he can, with what words he has and what gestures he can muster his bruised arms to, Inkin informs him; rolls his eyes, chutters and clucks and points to the southwest, where Grash-po-Nash is; points around to show that Laa'aa is gone. Blozzip's club lies on the floor of the cave. Inkin's bow is broken.

All this time, of course, Loof is at Carnack's heels; showing his teeth at the men at the caves; giving Moox a wide berth.

Carnack sets out at once, we may guess. It is out of the question for Inkin to go with him. He is too badly hurt.

On the way to The Haunt Starga intercepts him, where the trail crosses the river; creeps up through the grass, concealing herself from the others, stealing out of the caves on a pretext of hunting for berries, perhaps, or gathering roots, and waits for him there. Loof sniffs her and sounds the alarm, then knows who it is. Carnack brings up his bow. Starga stands up.

What does she tell him? She alone understands what has happened. She alone knows what has brought it about; the part she has played in it; the fury she brought on him, the vengeance on Laa'aa. Is that what she tells him? Does she suddenly see now, as she saw in the oaks that day when he came there with Loof—only more clearly—the light that is dawning for all in this man? Does the true woman in her begin now to see the true man in him, as Sarah saw what Isaac was and what Ishmael was not, as Rebekkah lifted Jacob up above his hairy brother, Mary conceived the Savior as an idea of God and another Mary was the first to see him risen from the cross?

That night, according to my computation, Carnack is far out in the basin where Grash-po-Nash is, swinging along, by the light of the moon and the glow of the volcano, toward the distant fiery peak. He has come up through The Haunt, gathering up all his weapons—his coup-de-poing made into an axe, his keen pointed spear, his arrows and bow. He turns his eyes toward the flare in the sky now and then, a night's walk away, or sweeps the vast shelving plain, filled with the mingled light of the milk-white moon and the blood-red fire, for sight, perhaps, of the sacrificial party.

There are three going thus through the night; Carnack and Loof and, trotting along, more or less at a distance, but always close enough to be keeping up with them, a horse, just turned past a colt, fine-limbed and well-bodied, a little wary of Loof, but otherwise wholly at ease and content.

Carnack is quite graphic in this scene, and in his description of their falling in with Pono, just over the ridge into Volcano Basin, as he and his dog came down from the head of Three-Quarters Cañon on the way to the plain—a spot, I should judge, not a hundred yards from where the overland auto road now passes.

No doubt the animal, so far off in the hills, was wandering alone, away from its fellows, in search of greener pastures. Or has it been led, as some suggest, by instinct, in the present critical juncture of nature, which extends to and includes Volcano

Basin, to the protection of this man's dominion, as Loof had been; or by a forgotten homing memory of one who had befriended and preserved it once before in an extremity? Has it a faint, suggestive reminiscence of him when it sees and senses him once more, as it comes trotting up the pass, tail up, head high, ears pricked, enormously inquisitive, attracted, frightened, bold, irresolute; or does it feel a strange, new security, some safe impulse of surrender, when it comes upon him, as it supposes, for the first time?

Carnack withholds his bow, appealed to, no doubt, by its trustfulness, and restrains Loof. They stand looking at each other, the three of them. Perhaps Carnack surmises. When he and Loof proceed Pono wheels and goes with them, swinging along in the moonlight and the glare of Grash-po-Nash.

Another night—the next one, probably—and we see Carnack standing on the slopes of Grash-po-Nash, the hot ground trembling under his naked feet, the earth roaring like a gigantic bison bull wounded with javelins, the fiery, seething rock below belching and sputtering and flopping in huge folds in the mighty throat of the monster, flames upflung and rolling canopies of smoke red with the fire beneath folding and unfolding in sinister bloody shadows, with now and then a mighty upward rushing spout of seething, hissing fire that comes down again in a rattling rain of burning rock. And overhead the moon.

What holds him there? How long does he stay? Is he only looking for the hunters from the hill? Is he only looking for Laa'aa? Or is he facing down the gods of his fathers, as he faced Old Huckar down that day on the rock at home when he was a naked boy; seeing through them, penetrating their smokey myth of fear and violence; knowing that this thing that seethes beneath him—mingled now with what once seemed Laa'aa—is the very thing that kept him warm throughout the winter that has gone; that makes his meat taste good; the servant and the friend of man?

He turns at last, we know from what follows, and heads for the little-used pass from Volcano Basin to The Valley of The Caves that crosses the ridge at the headwaters of Shoulder Hill Creek. That will take him home past the settlement. Perhaps he finds the trail of the others and follows them, for they, I think, returned that way. He travels all night, or the better part of it.

The next day—we must imagine this, knowing

what the rocks tell us later on—something comes
into the air; an impalpable softness. Its rigidity
breaks. It is not so vibrant and brittle. The tension goes out of the sky. In the morning a cloud
rises over the mountains to eastward, followed by
others; thin at first, just a tracery, a gossamer grey
in the glaring blue; then billowy piles, higher and
higher, spreading out, fold on fold, filling the sky-
line and mounting half way to the zenith.

Carnack reaches the head of the pass about nightfall, goes as far as he can, and stops for the night.
The moon swims in clouds, sinks into them, and is
lost. The stars are blotted out. He hears a restless breeze whisking from tree to tree in the cañon.
The dribble of water seems holding its breath. The
air is excited, expectant.

He starts down the cañon at daybreak; a rugged
descent, from boulder to boulder in the bed of the
stream, clinging to cliff sides, working his way
along ledges, weaving through thickets, swinging
up high over buttresses that close in on the chasm.
Loof is nimble and certain, and Pono scrambles
after.

The morning is cool. The sky is cast over—a
close, solid grey from mountain to mountain. The
trees turn up their leaves, holding out their hands,

their parched palms, to what is promised. A sense of moisture is present—a faint one, but certain.

The tops of the ridges are veiled. The cloud closes in. Its mist pours down the mountain sides, swirls into side cañons. The air is softened and melted.

It is afternoon when he gets to the caves. No doubt the mountain peaks and the cañons are crashing and rolling with thunder by the time he arrives.

A frenzy of joyous excitement has command of the people. They run up and down. They fling up their arms. Huckar is out with them. Carnack sees Starga sitting apart.

They catch sight of him and come toward him with menace. He wheels off and takes to the hills, heading for the trail to The Haunt. Blozzip whirls his club after him. Pono runs off. Loof stays close by, nervous and bristling.

A drop strikes his face, and another. He can hear the people shouting back at the caves. Some of them follow a distance. He has to send an arrow back at them.

He fringes the valley, keeping up in the hills to strike into the trail on Catamount Ridge.

The clouds lie flat above the lake, cutting sharp against the mountain walls that enclose the valley.

Here and there grey streaky curtains, high on the ridges, tell him that the rain has come. Lightning leaps. Thunder clatters mightily through the hills.

A long streamer of grey reaches down to the lake. The outlines of mountain and valley grow vague. The clearness, which lasted till now, goes out of the air. Now and then he still hears a faint shout from Shoulder Hill—a muffled, sinister murmur.

Then the air is ahush with a sigh, a deep, gasping sigh, and the rain comes, beating the leaves of the trees, splashing the rocks, getting them slowly wet, sinking at first into the ground, each drop disappearing, sucked swiftly away, then patches of dampness appear on the sand and the broken soil. The leaf mold glows and grows darker; the brooklets take heart. The hills open out and expand. Down comes the rain, verticle, even, soft and incessant, from low-lying clouds that catch on the mountain tops.

And so home to The Haunt, where Pono precedes and awaits them, and into the hut.

CHAPTER XX

EXODUS

NOTHING, perhaps, is more difficult to talk against than a superstition verified by circumstances. Those who adhere to it have the facts to point to. The Indian makes a decoction of herbs, gives it to a patient, and he is healed. Those observing it, believing beforehand that the patient would be healed, are convinced. Medical science, so-called, injects the blood of an unclean horse into the veins of a man believing, and making others believe, that it will protect him from this and that. He does not succumb to this or that, and the case is proven. A child comes home with its feet wet, and the mother tells it that it will take cold. Presently the child is sniffling and the mother is shown to be right. And so it goes, through the whole list, ancient and modern. How, then, could Carnack hope to explain to his people that the sacrifice of Laa'aa to the distant volcano and the coming of rain were a coincidence? How could he convince them that there was no relationship between facts so obviously associated with each other?

358

He could not, of course. Nor, indeed, would he have been entirely right if he could have done so. For the return of rain followed Laa'aa's atonement for Carnack's impertinence with fire as definitely and inevitably, through the belief of the people in it, as the efficacy of a drug follows its use through the popular superstition concerning it, or as water on the feet of a child makes the child sneeze because everybody—nearly—thinks that it will. Doubtless ghosts were as actual when believed in as influenza is today, and Salem witchcraft as real as modern microbes.

Nevertheless Carnack makes the attempt. How soon after the rain that Laa'aa brought he goes to them with fire to show them that it is good to them and does not drive the rain away, does not appear. It must have been a moon or two, at least. Prosperity, to all appearances, has returned to The Valley of The Caves and to the people in it. There must have been more rains than one, for we soon see the water lines in the sign of the waterfall increase from one to three. That, of course, could happen quickly in a mountain stream; but the grass in the little valley above the waterfall also flourishes again, and a summer green spreads through the bottom by the lake—thinly, to be sure, but definitely. The lake itself widens and fills. Rock-ribbed dells in the cañons turn dripping and verdant again. Deer reappear and feed on the ranges, elk roam the open places—in small bands, it is true—and the basin knows the bison and the horse once more. The hunters are out in the hills as before, the women chatter from the aprons of their caves, the children circulate through the woods and the fields in noisy bevies.

Carnack, we must conclude, stays close to The Haunt for the most part following the day of his return from Volcano Basin, when he has to take to the hill-side to avoid them and fling an admonitory arrow—if not an earnest one—after them. If he goes down to the caves to ply his trade in flints or on any other business he does not tell us. I think it extremely unlikely that he does. Why should he? Inkin has assumed full responsibility for the cave on Boulder Rock, and his own wants and Loof's can be easily supplied by their own hunting. Why go near the others? Why take the risk? Why provoke them? Why stir them up?

Cassell, indeed, insists that by this time even The Haunt would have become impossible for him; that the men from Shoulder Hill would not have stopped, after his sacrilege with fire, until they had quite driven him out or exterminated him. Primitives, he assures me, are like that. Sheer superstitious terror, he says, if nothing else, would have compelled them to rid themselves of anyone who brought such dreadful chances upon them. But I think he is wrong. The cave people of the Seafar Basin were too simple for that. Their fears, and therefore their hatreds, were too immediate and highly objective. They struck, and forgot. Until the next time.

Pono by this time has quite definitely joined the little group up behind the waterfall. We see him on the best of terms with them; browsing under their feet on the grass that the rain brings back, exchanging sniffs with Loof, pricking up his ears and nickering at Carnack, we can imagine, when Carnack turns out of his hut at daybreak or rises from the ground beneath the tree in the nook, where he may sleep in warmer weather.

Pono, we are informed, sometimes accompanies Loof and Carnack in their hunting, trotting along in front of them, or behind them, or in a wide sweep to the right or the left; stopping to graze and catching up on a gallop, stiff-legged, snorting, tail up; falling into a long trot, feet thrown well forward, head in the air.

Once we see Carnack putting the carcass of a deer on the young horse's back. See Pono, at last, trudging home under the burden, with Carnack marching beside him. It must have been a task to get the deer onto him; much snorting and sniffing; quick leaps aside, spilling the load half-way in the air; slow returns to Carnack's coaxing or commands, sniffing and snorting. Then the final cringe, with trembling knees and a battery of tiny snorts, and the first few quick steps under the load.

When Carnack begins to mount and ride him, strangely enough, he does not tell us, unless the one instance of it that we come to later is the first time. Men who know horses, and especially wild ones, tell me that would have been impossible. I do not know. I have only the pictures to go by. What might have been possible then, in the simplicity of time, we can leave to Carnack, perhaps, to tell us.

Meanwhile Carnack uses fire quite freely in The Haunt, to prepare his food, for he does not need it yet for warmth, and once he builds a fire for Inkin in front of the cave on Boulder Rock. He gives us the picture. Inkin, perhaps, has brought in a deer, or Carnack has, and Carnack proceeds to roast it, as he has learned how to do. Inkin has

PONO, THE YOUNG HORSE, BEARING A CARCASS OF DEER, WITH CARNACK MARCHING BESIDE HIM.

recovered from his defense of Laa'aa and the loss
of her, if it was a loss, and has taken a mate; some
daughter of the caves whom we have not seen before and cannot identify. She runs shrieking with
terror when she sees Carnack build up his little pile
of tinder and strike a spark into it until the fire
comes. Inkin has to go and retrieve her, half-way
up the cliff. Moox kicks over the fire and flies after
Loof, whom she blames for it. The two men build
up another, suppressing the women, and finish their
roasting. Inkin unquestionably learns how to make
fire and acquires the courage necessary to do it,
retaining both the knowledge and the assurance for
discreet revival, I have always thought, at a time
when the people of the caves, gradually dissolving
from the first hardening shock of Carnack's use of
it, are ready for it. It was no doubt through Inkin
that the knowledge was preserved for them, although we do not get a chance to see either him or
them employing it. We merely judge that they
did so, eventually, from signs found here and there
in the region showing its habitual use.

Why did Carnack go with fire to his people, late
that summer—if that is when he went? To save
other Laa'aas from the arms of Grash-po-Nash?
To bring them the blessing of its light and warmth,

of the way it would make meat taste for them? Or to make them see that it would not harm them, so that they would let him use it and not destroy him for it? He must have felt the danger he was in; the smouldering dread and fear of him amongst them, making every hour uncertain.

He draws the scene large and clearly for us. He is down in the oaks, in front of the caves, Loof at his side. Pono circles about at a distance, uneasy, disturbed, impatient, snorting and trotting and coming to stops, then wheeling off through the trees and back.

Carnack has his yellow hammerstone and his flints, and a handful of tinder, in a pouch he has made, a square of deer-skin, perhaps, tanned soft, and drawn together at the corners. He has picked up some pieces of bark on the way, and a few broken sticks.

He stops in an opening amongst the oaks, takes out his flints and his hammerstone, heaps up his tinder, squats down, strikes a spark, strikes another, into the little pile of powdery dust. The men are lined up. A deep hush falls over the people.

They hear the click of his flints, see him lean over and blow, and pile up small sticks. They see the smoke begin to curl up and flutter, see a flicker of flame, tiny at first, growing into a blaze.

He stands up and looks at them. He waves his arms at them, shouts to them in syllabic gutturals, trying to tell them. He points to the fire and makes gestures. Reaches down to the fire to show them how harmless it is.

A movement begins to run through them. A muttering murmur arises. They commence to come toward him, start howling and shouting. They sift down through the trees. Loof snarls and bristles, head down, showing his fangs. Pono leaps away, neighing and squealing in the distance.

Carnack slowly withdraws, leaving his fire.

Whether the men from Shoulder Hill pursue him at once, overhauling him in The Haunt, as Fischer insists that they did, or whether they work themselves up to it slowly, by stages—with Skihack's help, no doubt—and come later, the pictoliths have no way of telling us. Cassell gives Carnack an hour's retreat ahead of them. They would, he says, clinging to his false analogue of the cultivated savage of today whom he knows so well, mill and stew over the affair for a time, but only until they had worked themselves up sufficiently in their superstitious fears to face their fear of Carnack; who,

Cassell points out, would long since have become something mystic and occultly terrifying to them.

To that extent I think Cassell is right. The thought of Carnack frightened them. He did things they could not do and could not understand. They needed to fret themselves against him for the sake of their courage. But days, I think, intervene —Perigord agrees with me in this—two or three, perhaps, before they are ready to go; days while they slowly consider, with their dumb, sluggish faculties, the sequence and the consequence of what has occurred, holding one thing in mind at a time— the drought, Laa'aa, the trip to the volcano, the rain, Carnack's fire. Until his fire becomes at last the one thing at the bottom of it all, and they act, as the defensive life always acts, against the thing itself—in this case the man that does the thing— which is something it can see and understand, not seeing as the defensive life never sees, that the way to conquer fire is not to destroy the man that makes it but to take him in.

In any case it has been long enough for a sense of safety to have settled down and brooded in The Haunt. In the picture Carnack gives us of it just before the cave men come we feel a calm and quietude and peace which the place has never seemed to have before. It suggests, if anything could, relaxation and a belief—a false one, we are to see—of seclusion and security. Some find in it, too a sense of conclusion, the feeling of the setting sun and twilight, the quiet of the end.

This is the last picture but one—but two, strictly, for there is a companion to it—that we have of the spot, and the last one in which we see it still as it was in Carnack's time. The final view of it is one of desolation, after the men have wreaked upon it the vengeance and punishment which Carnack himself escapes.

In it we find Carnack sitting underneath his tree, idle. I imagine that the mood to do nothing was much upon him at this time. The lack of a mood to do anything, perhaps, would more accurately describe his state of mind. No doubt he was confused and baffled. No doubt he felt that his world was tumbling in upon his ears. No doubt he felt that The Haunt and The Valley of The Caves and Seafar Basin had become uninhabitable for him; that life there was ended and his work done. He was already driven out in mind and spirit.

But to give up fire, to renounce the bow and arrow, to drive off Loof and Pono and go back to live with the others in their noisy, nasty caves with a fat wife or two, we may be sure never occurred to him. One cannot give up the truth one has seen, one cannot turn back from the plow, even if one is a lonely cave man hunted through the rocks twenty thousand years and more before David fled from Saul, or the Savior, that great life-bringer, followed his vision to his cross—and the resurrection.

Loof is with him, lying close, with his nose across his master's lap. Carnack's hand is resting on the animal's shaggy head; the first and only instance we have of this. Carnack seems to be looking off at nothing. It is not difficult to think that his gaze may be trying to penetrate the years, the mystery of the resistance and the anger he has aroused against himself, harder than the rocks that intercept his gaze along the sides of the little valley where he has lived so long. It is not difficult to think that this is what he tries to tell us in this picture—which has no other purpose—; not so clearly, of course, as we can see it for him, but definitely enough to make us confident that something was stirring in his thoughts which could not be expressed in bow and arrows, cave men and women, flint chipping, fire building, or even carving on the rock.

How the peace of the scene is conveyed to us

across the stony face of twenty-five millenniums let
the artists and the psychologists of the day discuss.
Perhaps the quietude and serenity is partly in ourselves and our understanding of the man; but we
see it in the posture of the sitting figure, in his attitude, his ruminating gaze into space, the dog at his
side, the drape of the tree above, the sunlight on the
rocks, the little rivulet running from the lips of the
spring, in Pono grazing indolently down by the
brook.

We hear the low hum of a bee, the tiny, tinkling
plash of the spring, the flutter of small birds, busy
in the bushes, the sleepy whisper of the leaves,
awakened for a moment by a breeze wandering past
looking for company, Loof's deep breath of relaxation and contentment, the champing of Pono and
his little sneezes at the dust that gets in his nostrils,
the incessant, pleasant, restful rushing of the waterfall, the drone of the wind in the pines far off on
the ridges.

We feel the warm flow of air in amongst the
rocks, settling into cooler pools where the shadows
lie, tossing the grasses, combing its fingers through
Pono's mane and tail, exchanging confidences and
felicitations with the trees, lighting on the bush

tops, pressing soft on Carnack's cheek and naked arm and shoulder.

We smell the scents of ripened summer, of grasses gone to seed, of trees in their fruit, of dried and pungent leaves, firmly satisfied with duty done and ready to depart in the last splendor which is their reward and recompense, the spice of rock and shard and hillside, the aromatic redolence of conifers nearby, the vigorous odor of the wolf, the fragrance of the horse, sweet with new-cropped grass and freedom, and exhalations of the man himself clad in his skins and his integrity.

What lies beyond this place? What is there more?

Pono gives the alarm. Carnack hears him snort, sees him standing there for a moment in the last power of attention, looking down toward the waterfall where the trail climbs in, and come trotting excitedly toward the nook.

Loof, at the same moment, leaps to his feet, stifflegged, bristling, growling. Carnack runs down toward the brook, bow in hand, with a handful of arrows.

Here the second scene comes, companion to the first. We see the men from Shoulder Hill swarming up the little valley; Blozzip, Old Huckar, firm-footed again for the time, savage and mighty, brandishing his spear, roaring now that Carnack has discovered them, with the old light of the sun in his eye once more, the afterglow of sunset. Good Old Huckar. Doing his best as he sees it. Beside them, behind them, the others. Skihack and Skook and, I think, Heetow, are skirting the walls to encircle their victim—their bringer of life.

Carnack brings Skihack down with an arrow; drops him off from the rock like a partridge. He accounts for another, Heetow, if that is who it is, far advanced along the rocks at one side, well on his way behind Carnack. The others close in, courageous with terror and fury.

Loof takes a hand. Even Pono, charging amongst them, rearing and plunging, beating with hoofs, tearing with teeth, avoiding their spear-thrusts. Carnack goes down with the blow from a club, hurled by Blozzip, perhaps. The picture shows this. Skihack rolling off from his rock, transfixed with an arrow, Heetow crumpling up for a plunge to the ground below, Carnack lying prone, Pono in action, and Loof at the throat of The Hairy One; an instance, in drawing, of Carnack's handling of sequence as coincident in time— an effective, economical but confusing practice.

The next scene we must reconstruct for ourselves with nothing to build on, or with, but a third sketch, which some include with these other two in a trilogy, showing Carnack riding off on Pono's back up the gorge at the head of the little valley with his pursuers left behind; a picture which has aroused a storm as great as any in the pictoliths. It cannot, however, be repudiated. Incredulity has not that easy escape. Carnack drew it, and Carnack had not learned how to lie. Deception is deliberate self-interest, and that came much later in the life of man.

So we may see him lying there, felled by a club, stunned, with the others closing in upon him, Loof snapping and slashing at them, Pono beating them down with his hoofs, javelins in the air, and now and then a club swinging in its parabola across the scene; Carnack trying to come back and recover himself. We can hear the shouting and the triumph and the hate; Old Huckar's roar, Blozzip's bellow from his bloody throat, torn by Loof, the shriller shriek of Palupe coming to his ears as he lies there, floating between consciousness and oblivion, braced for the next stroke, and perhaps the final one; feeling the life surging back slowly, awaiting the issue.

We must picture his companions running to him in a respite, the enemy at bay for the moment; Loof sniffing and panting on him, nosing him, poking him with vigorous affection and concern; Pono nickering and sniffing, pawing the ground, wheeling on his front feet to keep an eye on the others, gathering themselves and their weapons to resume the attack. See the horse kneel down, perhaps, or perhaps not. See Carnack struggle to his elbow, to his knees, to his feet, clinging to the horse's shoulder and mane, see him clamber to the back of the animal, note Pono's quick leap, note Loof holding off the first stage of pursuit, see Pono gallop up the shelving slope of the little valley, twist out of sight for a moment around the first point, and climb nimbly up the gorge at its head with strong limbs and arched back and many leg-thrusts against crunching shard and flinty rock and soft, yielding soil; hear the angry cry of the men deprived of their object, hear missiles in the air, observe the first few steps of pursuit, its reliquishment, their fury turned upon each other and The Haunt, as Pono, with Carnack clinging to his back and Loof convoying them against possible surprise in the rocks or bushes, makes his way to the head of the gorge and so into Three-Quarters Cañon and the pass to Volcano Basin. We must picture some such scene as this for ourselves, because we have the conclusion of it in the little sketch immediately following the one in which Carnack has been laid low; Pono and Carnack and Loof mounting the gulch as has been described.

There is one more picture of The Haunt.

What brings Carnack back—whether he returns to gather up his bow and hammerstones and flint and tinder, or with the hope, perhaps, of staying there, or whether he is drawn by a desire for a last look at the place and a proper departure from it— and how soon he returns, we cannot tell, but we see him there again, standing in the midst of its desolation. Failing him, they have fallen upon the place and bestrewed it with its wreckage. Nothing is left of the hut. Not even a standing pole or a single stone in place. Only a heap where it stood, and a small one, for most of it they scattered with infuriated foot and club and spear. They have beaten down bushes, they have torn at the spring, they have gashed the very tree that shaded him. No doubt they showered blows upon the rock behind it, and I have always been convinced that this was the time when one of them, most likely Blozzip, went around the buttress that shut off the bench where

STARGA AND CARNACK CROSSED THE PLAIN BY NIGHT WITH
THE STAR OF THEIR NEW LOVE LEADING THEM ON.

Carnack wrought his pictoliths and made a ferocious scratch upon them; their only disfigurement. His bow, although he does not show it, is undoubtedly in splinters; his arrows broken into bits, his arrowheads and spearheads and his hammerstones strewn to the winds, his spears reduced to twisted slivers. Thus hatred would destroy idea, and cannot; for other bows are bent by him, we know, and other flint heads take form from out the heart of stones, and other arrows taper into shape beneath his hand, directed by the thought that has come and cannot recede again into that great reservoir from which it flowed.

Now someone is coming. Pono looks up from his browsing, midrib of the glen, snorting softly, walks off in a circle, and stands. Loof woofs, then sniffs and subsides, with a glance up at Carnack.

Carnack hears the approach, hears footsteps through grass, sees Pono's eyes following, tracing the progress of the one who is coming.

She comes around the rock and stands there before him in what was his nook.

They gaze at each other.

Starga smiles.

As Eve conceived Abel and Seth, as Sarah bore Isaac in wisdom, as Rebekah perceived Israel in

Jacob and uplifted him, as the Virgin beheld and brought forth God's ideal of man which is the savior of all men, so now the true woman in Starga, awakened at last to the vision, sees the true man in this man and shields it and loves it, evokes it and raises it up, completing, perfecting, fulfilling, sufficing; unfolding for both that full image and likeness of God which He created male and female, and saw to be good, before ever Adam was or Eve took form in a dream from a rib.

This, at least, is my interpretation of the picture. The scientists and experts, quite naturally, have others. Mine is out of their field. At the same time Perigord. . . .

We have only one more picture. Starga and Carnack. Crossing, by night, under the star-crusted sky, the plain of the basin where Grashpo-Nash was. With the star of their new love leading them on. Taking between them "the young child" into Egypt, the dawning vision of true union, away from the caves and The Haunt, away from the Herods of ignorance and fear and brutality that would know it only to destroy it, and them with it. Carnack and Starga. Out under the sky and the stars. With their faces in the starlight. Loof at their heels. Pono trotting beside them.

THE END

CPSIA information can be obtained
at www.ICGtesting.com
Printed in the USA
BVOW06s1939310117
474967BV00017B/280/P